Diabetic Air Fryer
Cookbook for Beginners 2023

1800

Healthy, Easy and Mouthwatering Low-Glycemic Recipes, Manage and Enjoy Your Life's Journey with Diabetes, Includes 4 Weeks Meal Plans

Brandee Reyes

CONTENTS

Chapter 4: Poultry Recipes.. 36

Chapter 5: Beef, Pork And Lamb Recipes.................................... 50

Chapter 6: Fish And Seafood Recipes...................................... 65

Chapter 7: Other Favorite Recipes 79

4-Week Meal Plan 95

Appendix : Recipes Index 99

INTRODUCTION

Diabetes mellitus, popularly referred to as just Diabetes, is a chronic condition that causes a person's blood glucose to become too high. 100,000 people die each year from the disease In the U.S. alone. And it's a steadily increasing number, recent studies show. Scientists also claim that unless we do something about it, by 2025 there will be a 33% increase in deaths due to this "silent killer", so what can we do?

As a matter of fact, here you will find how to prevent and curb the disease, whether you have prediabetes or type 2 diabetes. My name is Brandee Reyes, My first resolution after the type 2 diabetes diagnosis last year was to reform my diet fully. One of my biggest concerns was how to adjust my cooking practices. And to fast-track my new diabetes lifestyle, the first recommendation was the best air fryer for diabetics . Will an air fryer help a diabetic? It's a commonly asked question.

In short, an air fryer is not a miracle cure for diabetes. However, it can help you improve your diet as a diabetic and prepare food with less oil. If you are reading this page, it means that you have already decided to start a better Lifestyle. This book contains 1800 diabetes recipes simplify meal planning for individuals who live with diabetes. They allow home cooks to focus on cooking instead of research.

If you don't know how to start this new diet pattern, you might as well try the 4 weeks diet plan in the cookbook first. After trying it, I believe you will love this healthy and simple diet.

Are you ready?

Let's dive right into it.

Chapter 1: Diabetic Air Fryer Diet

Understanding Diabetes

Diabetes is a disease that occurs when your blood glucose, also called blood sugar, is too high. Blood glucose is your main source of energy and comes from the food you eat. This metabolic disease can affect the entire body and if complications develop, diabetes can have adverse effects on the impact of life and can decrease life expectancy. Although diabetes has no cure, you can take steps to manage your diabetes and stay healthy.

To understand diabetes better, it's vital that you understand the role of insulin in the body. Insulin, a hormone made by the pancreas, helps glucose from food get into your cells to be used for energy. When you eat food, your body turns the food into glucose. The pancreas is triggered to release insulin that opens your cells to let the glucose enter. This is the same glucose that is used for energy. Sometimes your body doesn't make enough insulin. Glucose then stays in your blood and doesn't reach your cells. Over time, having high glucose levels can cause health problems.

Types of Diabetes

The most common types of diabetes are type 1 and type 2. While they may sound like the same thing, they certainly are not. Let me elaborate further. To start with, both share the same problem: high blood glucose levels.

Air fryers actually seem to produce lower amounts of acrylamide. Indeed, a 2015 study published in the Journal of Food Science found that air-fried fries had 90% less acrylamide than deep-fried fries.

(2) Air fryers reduce calories

As mentioned before, another advantage of air fryers is that they reduce calories, because they don't require as much oil. For example, air-fried foods can require only one teaspoon of oil – that's just 40 calories.

Conversely, a single tablespoon of oil absorbed into food during ordinary frying adds about 120 calories. Therefore, replacing deep-fried foods with air-fried foods can help with weight management.

(3) Air fryers do not produce some of the toxic compounds found in deep-fried foods

There is another benefit made possible by reducing oil use. For example, when oil is reused for deep-frying (as often happens in restaurants), its quality decreases, depleting the food of antioxidants and producing harmful chemicals. Therefore, eating foods without antioxidants compromises the body's antioxidant defense system, increasing the risk of disease. It may also cause inflammation of the blood vessels (which reduces the blood flow) and hypertension.

This far, you've seen what an air fryer is, how it works, and why you should use it. In the next section, we'll go back to food choices related to diabetes, and especially What foods should people with diabetes avoid.

Type 1 Diabetes

Type 1 diabetes is thought to be caused by an autoimmune reaction (the body attacks itself by mistake). Your immune system attacks and destroys the cells in your pancreas that make insulin. Symptoms of type 1 diabetes often develop quickly. It's usually diagnosed in children and young adults. Symptoms include excessive excretion of urine (polyuria), thirst (polydipsia), constant hunger, weight loss, vision changes, and fatigue. These symptoms may occur suddenly. People with type 1 diabetes need daily insulin to stay alive.

Type 2 Diabetes

Type 2 diabetes results from the body's ineffective use of insulin. It usually occurs in middle-aged adults, most often 40+ and accounts for the majority of diabetes cases (90 percent). This type of diabetes is largely the result of excess body weight and physical inactivity. Additionally, having type 2 diabetes poses very high risks of the emergence of cardiovascular disease and other types of health disorders. Ensuring a healthy diet and increased physical activity are two lifestyle changes that can help you keep your blood glucose levels in check.

Can Diabetics Eat Air Fried Food?

This is really important so let's see what the 3 reasons are:

(1) Air fryers reduce the amount of acrylamide in food

Deep-fried foods contain high amounts of acrylamide – a substance that forms when carbohydrates are heated to high temperatures – which has been linked to heart disease.

In fact, the Department of Health and Human Services defines acrylamide as "carcinogenic to humans" and based on recent animal studies, they have concluded that this can even lead to cancer. However, more research is needed, according to the National Cancer Institute. What's the good news?

What Foods Should People with Diabetes Avoid?

(1) Sugary drinks

Sugary drinks are harmful to diabetic patients since they are very high in carbohydrates. In fact, a 12-ounce (354 ml) can of Coke, contains 38.5 grams of carbs. Similarly, sweetened iced tea contains almost 45 grams of carbohydrates. Plus these beverages are rich in fructose, which is strongly linked to insulin resistance and diabetes.

(2) Trans Fat

Fats are bad for your diabetes. Specifically, they are related to increased inflammation, insulin resistance, and belly fat, as well as lower levels of HDL (good) cholesterol and reduced arterial function. Did you know that trans fats are banned in most countries? And in 2018 the Food and Drug Administration (FDA) banned the use of partially hydrogenated oil, which is the main source of trans fats.

(3) White bread, rice, and pasta

Eating bread, bagels, and other refined flour foods has been shown to significantly increase blood sugar levels in people with type 1 and type 2 diabetes. In one study, gluten-free kinds of pasta were also found to increase blood sugar, with rice-based varieties having the greatest effect.

(4) Honey

People with diabetes tend to cut down on white sugar. However, other forms of sugar can also cause blood sugar spikes. These include brown sugar and "natural" sugars such as honey, as well as agave nectar and maple syrup. Although these sweeteners are not highly processed, they contain at least as many carbohydrates like white sugar. Your best strategy is to avoid all forms of sugar and use low-carb natural sweeteners instead - or better still, none at all.

(5) Packaged snacks

Snacking on pretzels, crackers or other packaged savory snacks is not healthy for people with prediabetes or diabetes. In fact, these products are generally made from refined flour and provide few nutrients, while having many fast-digesting carbohydrates that can rapidly spike blood sugar. Just think, one study found that snacks provide an average of 7.7% more carbohydrates than what they claim on their labels. And depending on the size of the packaging, controlling the portion of these snacks that they eat is a challenge for lots of people.

That's why choosing to cook with an air fryer may be the best choice you can make.

BASIC KITCHEN CONVERSIONS & EQUIVALENTS

DRY MEASUREMENTS CONVERSION CHART

3 TEASPOONS = 1 TABLESPOON = 1/16 CUP

6 TEASPOONS = 2 TABLESPOONS = 1/8 CUP

12 TEASPOONS = 4 TABLESPOONS = 1/4 CUP

24 TEASPOONS = 8 TABLESPOONS = 1/2 CUP

36 TEASPOONS = 12 TABLESPOONS = 3/4 CUP

48 TEASPOONS = 16 TABLESPOONS = 1 CUP

METRIC TO US COOKING CONVERSIONS

OVEN TEMPERATURES

120 °C = 250 °F

160 °C = 320 °F

180° C = 350 °F

205 °C = 400 °F

220 °C = 425 °F

LIQUID MEASUREMENTS CONVERSION CHART

8 FLUID OUNCES = 1 CUP = 1/2 PINT = 1/4 QUART

16 FLUID OUNCES = 2 CUPS = 1 PINT = 1/2 QUART

32 FLUID OUNCES = 4 CUPS = 2 PINTS = 1 QUART

= 1/4 GALLON

128 FLUID OUNCES = 16 CUPS = 8 PINTS = 4 QUARTS = 1 GALLON

BAKING IN GRAMS

1 CUP FLOUR = 140 GRAMS

1 CUP SUGAR = 150 GRAMS

1 CUP POWDERED SUGAR = 160 GRAMS

1 CUP HEAVY CREAM = 235 GRAMS

VOLUME

1 MILLILITER = 1/5 TEASPOON

5 ML = 1 TEASPOON

15 ML = 1 TABLESPOON

240 ML = 1 CUP OR 8 FLUID OUNCES

1 LITER = 34 FL. OUNCES

WEIGHT

1 GRAM = .035 OUNCES

100 GRAMS = 3.5 OUNCES

500 GRAMS = 1.1 POUNDS

1 KILOGRAM = 35 OUNCES

US TO METRIC COOKING CONVERSIONS

1/5 TSP = 1 ML

1 TSP = 5 ML

1 TBSP = 15 ML

1 FL OUNCE = 30 ML

1 CUP = 237 ML

1 PINT (2 CUPS) = 473 ML

1 QUART (4 CUPS) = .95 LITER

1 GALLON (16 CUPS) = 3.8 LITERS

1 OZ = 28 GRAMS

1 POUND = 454 GRAMS

BUTTER

1 CUP BUTTER = 2 STICKS = 8 OUNCES = 230 GRAMS = 8 TABLESPOONS

WHAT DOES 1 CUP EQUAL

1 CUP = 8 FLUID OUNCES

1 CUP = 16 TABLESPOONS

1 CUP = 48 TEASPOONS

1 CUP = 1/2 PINT

1 CUP = 1/4 QUART

1 CUP = 1/16 GALLON

1 CUP = 240 ML

BAKING PAN CONVERSIONS

1 CUP ALL-PURPOSE FLOUR = 4.5 OZ

1 CUP ROLLED OATS = 3 OZ 1 LARGE EGG = 1.7 OZ

1 CUP BUTTER = 8 OZ 1 CUP MILK = 8 OZ

1 CUP HEAVY CREAM = 8.4 OZ

1 CUP GRANULATED SUGAR = 7.1 OZ

1 CUP PACKED BROWN SUGAR = 7.75 OZ

1 CUP VEGETABLE OIL = 7.7 OZ

1 CUP UNSIFTED POWDERED SUGAR = 4.4 OZ

BAKING PAN CONVERSIONS

9-INCH ROUND CAKE PAN = 12 CUPS

10-INCH TUBE PAN =16 CUPS

11-INCH BUNDT PAN = 12 CUPS

9-INCH SPRINGFORM PAN = 10 CUPS

9 X 5 INCH LOAF PAN = 8 CUPS

9-INCH SQUARE PAN = 8 CUPS

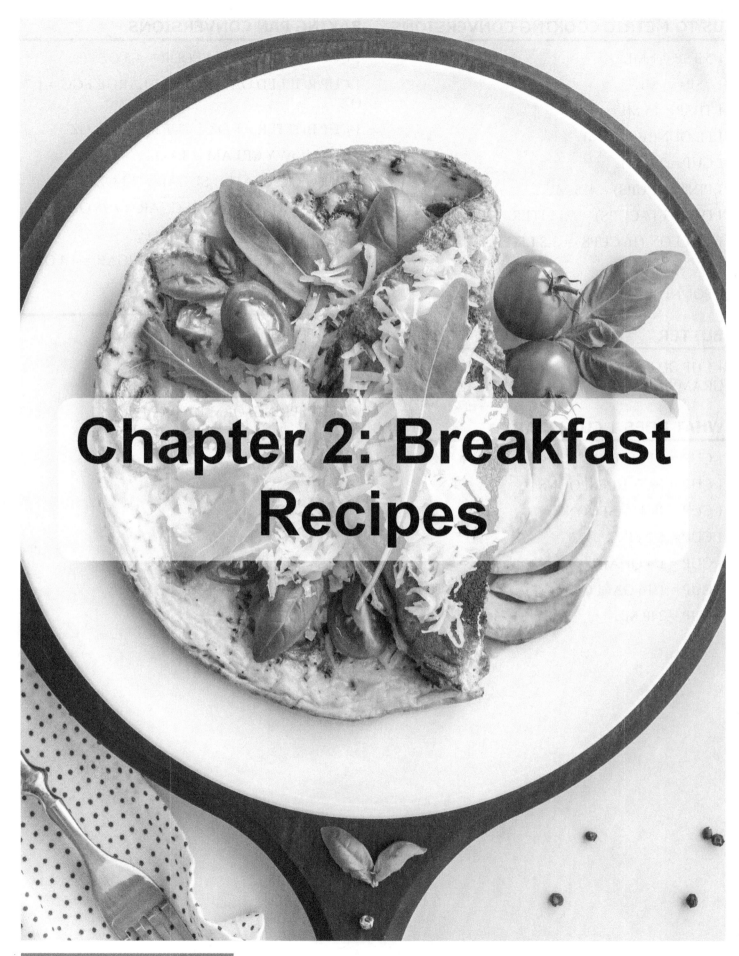

Chapter 2: Breakfast Recipes

Chapter 2: Breakfast Recipes

Santa Fe Style Pizza

Servings: Two | Cooking Time: 10 Minutes

Ingredients:

- 1 tsp. vegetable oil
- ½ tsp. ground cumin
- 2 tortillas 7 to 8 inches in diameter
- ¼ cup black bean sauce prepared
- 4 ounces cooked chicken, in strips or grated
- 1 tbsp. taco seasonings
- 2 tbsp. prepared chipotle sauce, or preferred sauce
- ¼ cup plus 2 tbsp. corn kernels, fresh or frozen (thawed)
- 1 tbsp. sliced scallions
- 1 tsp. chopped cilantro
- ⅔ cup grated pepper jack cheese

Directions:

1. Put the oil with the cumin in a small bowl; spread the mixture on both tortillas. Then spread the black bean sauce evenly over both tortillas. Put the chicken pieces and taco seasonings in medium bowl; Stir until chicken is covered. Add the sauce and mix it with the covered chicken.
2. Remove half of the chicken and place it over the bean sauce in one of the tortillas. Put half the corn, chives, and cilantro over the tortilla and then cover with half the cheese. Put the pizza inside the basket and cook it at a temperature of 400°F for 10 minutes. Prepare the other tortilla and cook it after removing the first one.

Nutrition Info:

- Calories: 41 Fat: 1.01g Carbohydrates: 6.68g Protein: 1.08g Sugar: 0.25g Cholesterol: 0mg

Pancakes

Servings: 4 | Cooking Time: 29 Minutes

Ingredients:

- 1 1/2 cup coconut flour
- 1 teaspoon salt
- 3 1/2 teaspoons baking powder
- 1 tablespoon erythritol sweetener
- 1 1/2 teaspoon baking soda
- 3 tablespoons melted butter
- 1 1/4 cups milk, unsweetened, reduced-fat
- 1 egg, pastured

Directions:

1. Switch on the air fryer, insert fryer pan, grease it with olive oil, then shut with its lid, set the fryer at 220 degrees F and preheat for 5 minutes.
2. Meanwhile, take a medium bowl, add all the ingredients in it, whisk until well blended and then let the mixture rest for 5 minutes.

3. Open the fryer, pour in some of the pancake mixture as thin as possible, close with its lid and cook for 6 minutes until nicely golden, turning the pancake halfway through the frying.
4. When air fryer beeps, open its lid, transfer pancake onto a serving plate and use the remaining batter for cooking more pancakes in the same manner.
5. Serve straight away with fresh fruits slices.

Nutrition Info:

- Calories: 237.7 CalCarbs: 39.2 gFat: 10.2 gProtein: 6.3 gFiber: 1.3 g

Cream Buns With Strawberries

Servings: 6 | Cooking Time: 12 Minutes

Ingredients:

- 240g all-purpose flour
- 50g granulated sugar
- 8g baking powder
- 1g of salt
- 85g chopped cold butter
- 84g chopped fresh strawberries
- 120 ml whipping cream
- 2 large eggs
- 10 ml vanilla extract
- 5 ml of water

Directions:

1. Sift flour, sugar, baking powder and salt in a large bowl. Put the butter with the flour using a blender or your hands until the mixture resembles thick crumbs.
2. Mix the strawberries in the flour mixture. Set aside for the mixture to stand. Beat the whipping cream, 1 egg and the vanilla extract in a separate bowl.
3. Put the cream mixture in the flour mixture until they are homogeneous, then spread the mixture to a thickness of 38 mm.
4. Use a round cookie cutter to cut the buns. Spread the buns with a combination of egg and water. Set aside
5. Preheat the air fryer, set it to 180°C.
6. Place baking paper in the preheated inner basket.
7. Place the buns on top of the baking paper and cook for 12 minutes at 180°C, until golden brown.

Nutrition Info:

- Calories: 150Fat: 14g Carbohydrates: 3g Protein: 11g Sugar: 8g Cholesterol: 0mg

Bruschetta

Servings: 2 | Cooking Time: 10 Minutes

Ingredients:

- 4 slices of Italian bread
- 1 cup chopped tomato tea
- 1 cup grated mozzarella tea
- Olive oil
- Oregano, salt, and pepper
- 4 fresh basil leaves

Directions:

1. Preheat the air fryer. Set the timer of 5 minutes and the temperature to 2000C.
2. Sprinkle the slices of Italian bread with olive oil. Divide the chopped tomatoes and mozzarella between the slices. Season with salt, pepper, and oregano.
3. Put oil in the filling. Place a basil leaf on top of each slice.
4. Put the bruschetta in the basket of the air fryer being careful not to spill the filling. Set the timer of 5 minutes, set the temperature to 180C, and press the power button.
5. Transfer the bruschetta to a plate and serve.

Nutrition Info:

- Calories: 434 Fat: 14g Carbohydrates: 63g Protein: 11g Sugar: 8g Cholesterol: 0mg

Misto Quente

Servings: 4 | Cooking Time: 10 Minutes

Ingredients:

- 4 slices of bread without shell
- 4 slices of turkey breast
- 4 slices of cheese
- 2 tbsp. cream cheese
- 2 spoons of butter

Directions:

1. Preheat the air fryer. Set the timer of 5 minutes and the temperature to 200C.
2. Pass the butter on one side of the slice of bread, and on the other side of the slice, the cream cheese.
3. Mount the sandwiches placing two slices of turkey breast and two slices cheese between the breads, with the cream cheese inside and the side with butter.
4. Place the sandwiches in the basket of the air fryer. Set the timer of the air fryer for 5 minutes and press the power button.

Nutrition Info:

- Calories: 340 Fat: 15g Carbohydrates: 32g Protein: 15g Sugar: 0g Cholesterol: 0mg

Cauliflower Hash Browns

Servings: 6 | Cooking Time: 25 Minutes

Ingredients:

- 1/4 cup chickpea flour
- 4 cups cauliflower rice
- 1/2 medium white onion, peeled and chopped
- 1/2 teaspoon garlic powder
- 1 tablespoon xanthan gum
- 1/2 teaspoon salt
- 1 tablespoon nutritional yeast flakes
- 1 teaspoon ground paprika

Directions:

1. Switch on the air fryer, insert fryer basket, grease it with olive oil, then shut with its lid, set the fryer at 375 degrees F and preheat for 10 minutes.
2. Meanwhile, place all the ingredients in a bowl, stir until well mixed and then shape the mixture into six rectangular disks, each about ½-inch thick.
3. Open the fryer, add hash browns in it in a single layer, close with its lid and cook for 25 minutes at the 375 degrees F until nicely golden and crispy, turning halfway through the frying.
4. When air fryer beeps, open its lid, transfer hash browns to a serving plate and serve.

Nutrition Info:

- Calories: 115.2 CalCarbs: 6.2 gFat: 7.3 gProtein: 7.4 gFiber: 2.2 g

Sweet Nuts Butter

Servings: 5 | Cooking Time: 25 Minutes

Ingredients:

- 1½ pounds sweet potatoes, peeled and cut into ½ inch pieces (2 medium)
- ½ tbsp. olive oil
- 1 tbsp. melted butter
- 1 tbsp. finely chopped walnuts
- ½ tsp. grated one orange
- ⅛ tsp. nutmeg
- ⅛ tsp. ground cinnamon

Directions:

1. Put sweet potatoes in a small bowl and sprinkle with oil. Stir until covered and then pour into the basket, ensuring that they are in a single layer. Cook at a temperature of 350°F for 20 to 25 minutes, stirring or turning halfway through cooking. Remove them to the serving plate. Combine the butter, nuts, orange zest, nutmeg, and cinnamon in a small bowl and pour the mixture over the sweet potatoes.

Nutrition Info:

- Calories: 141 Fat: 1.01g Carbohydrates: 6.68g Protein: 1.08g Sugar: 0.25g Cholesterol: 7mg

Grilled Cheese

Servings: 2 | Cooking Time: 7 Minutes

Ingredients:

- 4 slices brown bread
- 1/2 cup shredded sharp cheddar cheese
- 1/4 cup melted butter

Directions:

1. Adjust your air fryer to 360°F.
2. In separate bowls, place cheese and butter.
3. Melt butter and brush it onto the 4 slices of bread.
4. Place cheese on 2 sides of bread slices.
5. Put sandwiches together and place them into the cooking basket.
6. Cook for 5 minutes and serve warm.

Nutrition Info:

- Calories: 214 kcal Total Fat: 11.2g Carbs: 9.4g Protein: 13.2g

Scotch Eggs

Servings: 4 | Cooking Time: 15 Minutes

Ingredients:

- 1-pound pork sausage, pastured
- 2 tablespoons chopped parsley
- 1/8 teaspoon salt
- 1/8 teaspoon grated nutmeg
- 1 tablespoon chopped chives
- 1/8 teaspoon ground black pepper
- 2 teaspoons ground mustard, and more as needed
- 4 eggs, hard-boiled, shell peeled
- 1 cup shredded parmesan cheese, low-fat

Directions:

1. Switch on the air fryer, insert fryer basket, grease it with olive oil, then shut with its lid, set the fryer at 400 degrees F and preheat for 10 minutes.
2. Meanwhile, place sausage in a bowl, add salt, black pepper, parsley, chives, nutmeg, and mustard, then stir until well mixed and shape the mixture into four patties.
3. Peel each boiled egg, then place an egg on a patty and shape the meat around it until the egg has evenly covered.
4. Place cheese in a shallow dish, and then roll the egg in the cheese until covered completely with cheese; prepare remaining eggs in the same manner.
5. Then open the fryer, add eggs in it, close with its lid and cook for 15 minutes at the 400 degrees F until nicely golden and crispy, turning the eggs and spraying with oil halfway through the frying.
6. When air fryer beeps, open its lid, transfer eggs onto a serving plate and serve with mustard.

Nutrition Info:

- Calories: 533 CalCarbs: 2 gFat: 43 gProtein: 33 gFiber: 1 g

Zucchini Bread

Servings: 8 | Cooking Time: 40 Minutes

Ingredients:

- ¾ cup shredded zucchini
- 1/2 cup almond flour
- 1/4 teaspoon salt
- 1/4 cup cocoa powder, unsweetened
- 1/2 cup chocolate chips, unsweetened, divided
- 6 tablespoons erythritol sweetener
- 1/2 teaspoon baking soda
- 2 tablespoons olive oil
- 1/2 teaspoon vanilla extract, unsweetened
- 2 tablespoons butter, unsalted, melted
- 1 egg, pastured

Directions:

1. Switch on the air fryer, insert fryer basket, grease it with olive oil, then shut with its lid, set the fryer at 310 degrees F and preheat for 10 minutes.
2. Meanwhile, place flour in a bowl, add salt, cocoa powder, and baking soda and stir until mixed.
3. Crack the eggs in another bowl, whisk in sweetener, egg, oil, butter, and vanilla until smooth and then slowly whisk in flour mixture until incorporated.
4. Add zucchini along with 1/3 cup chocolate chips and then fold until just mixed.
5. Take a mini loaf pan that fits into the air fryer, grease it with olive oil, then pour in the prepared batter and sprinkle remaining chocolate chips on top.
6. Open the fryer, place the loaf pan in it, close with its lid and cook for 30 minutes at the 310 degrees F until inserted toothpick into the bread slides out clean.
7. When air fryer beeps, open its lid, remove the loaf pan, then place it on a wire rack and let the bread cool in it for 20 minutes.
8. Take out the bread, let it cool completely, then cut it into slices and serve.

Nutrition Info:

- Calories: 356 CalCarbs: 49 gFat: 17 gProtein: 5.1 gFiber: 2.5 g

Tofu Scramble

Servings: 3 | Cooking Time: 18 Minutes

Ingredients:

- 12 ounces tofu, extra-firm, drained, ½-inch cubed
- 1 teaspoon garlic powder
- 1 teaspoon onion powder
- 1 teaspoon paprika
- 1/2 teaspoon ground black pepper
- 1/2 teaspoon salt
- 1 tablespoon olive oil
- 2 teaspoon xanthan gum

Directions:

1. Switch on the air fryer, insert fryer basket, grease it with olive oil, then shut with its lid, set the fryer at 220 degrees F and preheat for 5 minutes.
2. Meanwhile, place tofu pieces in a bowl, drizzle with oil, and sprinkle with xanthan gum and toss until well coated.
3. Add remaining ingredients to the tofu and then toss until well coated.
4. Open the fryer, add tofu in it, close with its lid and cook for 13 minutes until nicely golden and crispy, shaking the basket every 5 minutes.
5. When air fryer beeps, open its lid, transfer tofu onto a serving plate and serve.

Nutrition Info:

- Calories: 94 CalCarbs: 5 gFat: 5 gProtein: 6 gFiber: 0 g

Morning Mini Cheeseburger Sliders

Servings: 6 | Cooking Time: 10minutes

Ingredients:

- 1 lb. ground beef
- 6 slices cheddar cheese
- 6 dinner rolls
- Salt and Black pepper

Directions:

1. Adjust the air fryer to 390°F.
2. Form 6 beef patties (each about 5 oz.) and season with salt and black pepper.
3. Add the burger patties to the cooking basket and cook them for 10 minutes.
4. Place bun and the cheese and cook for another minute.

Nutrition Info:

- Calories: 262 kcal Total Fat: 9.4g Carbs: 8.2g Protein: 16.2g

Blueberry Buns

Servings: 6 | Cooking Time: 12 Minutes

Ingredients:

- 240g all-purpose flour
- 50g granulated sugar
- 8g baking powder
- 2g of salt
- 85g chopped cold butter
- 85g of fresh blueberries
- 3g grated fresh ginger
- 113 ml whipping cream
- 2 large eggs
- 4 ml vanilla extract
- 5 ml of water

Directions:

1. Put sugar, flour, baking powder and salt in a large bowl.
2. Put the butter with the flour using a blender or your hands until the mixture resembles thick crumbs.
3. Mix the blueberries and ginger in the flour mixture and

set aside
4. Mix the whipping cream, 1 egg and the vanilla extract in a different container.
5. Put the cream mixture with the flour mixture until combined.
6. Shape the dough until it reaches a thickness of approximately 38 mm and cut it into eighths.
7. Spread the buns with a combination of egg and water. Set aside Preheat the air fryer set it to 180°C.
8. Place baking paper in the preheated inner basket and place the buns on top of the paper. Cook for 12 minutes at 180°C, until golden brown

Nutrition Info:

- Calories: 105 Fat: 1.64g Carbohydrates: 20.09gProtein: 2.43g Sugar: 2.1g Cholesterol: 0mg

Blueberry Muffins

Servings: 14 | Cooking Time: 30 Minutes

Ingredients:

- 1 cup almond flour
- 1 cup frozen blueberries
- 2 teaspoons baking powder
- 1/3 cup erythritol sweetener
- 1 teaspoon vanilla extract, unsweetened
- ½ teaspoon salt
- ¼ cup melted coconut oil
- 1 egg, pastured
- ¼ cup applesauce, unsweetened
- ¼ cup almond milk, unsweetened

Directions:

1. Switch on the air fryer, insert fryer basket, grease it with olive oil, then shut with its lid, set the fryer at 360 degrees F and preheat for 10 minutes.
2. Meanwhile, place flour in a large bowl, add berries, salt, sweetener, and baking powder and stir until well combined.
3. Crack the eggs in another bowl, whisk in vanilla, milk, and applesauce until combined and then slowly whisk in flour mixture until incorporated.
4. Take fourteen silicone muffin cups, grease them with oil, and then evenly fill them with the prepared batter.
5. Open the fryer, stack muffin cups in it, close with its lid and cook for 10 minutes until muffins are nicely golden brown and set.
6. When air fryer beeps, open its lid, transfer muffins onto a serving plate and then remaining muffins in the same manner.
7. Serve straight away.

Nutrition Info:

- Calories: 201 CalCarbs: 27.3 gFat: 8.8 gProtein: 3 gFiber: 1.2 g

Grilled Sandwich With Three Types Of Cheese

Servings: Two | Cooking Time: 8 Minutes

Ingredients:

- 2 tbsp. mayonnaise
- ⅛ tsp. dried basil
- ⅛ tsp. dried oregano
- 4 slices of whole wheat bread
- 2 slices of ½ to 1-ounce cheddar cheese
- 2 slices of Monterey Jack cheese
- ½ to 1 ounce
- 2 thin slices of tomato
- 2 slices of ½ to 1 oz. provolone cheese Soft butter

Directions:

1. Mix mayonnaise with basil and oregano in a small bowl and then spread the mixture on each side of the slice. Cover each slice with a slice of each cheese and tomato, and then the other slice of bread.
2. Lightly brush each side of the sandwich and put the sandwiches in the basket. Cook at a temperature of 400°F for 8 minutes, turning halfway through cooking.

Nutrition Info:

- Calories: 141 Fat: 1.01g Carbohydrates: 68g Protein: 1.08g Sugar: 0.25g Cholesterol: 33mg

Air Fried Sausage

Servings: 2 | Cooking Time: 14 Minutes

Ingredients:

- 2-3 thick sausages

Directions:

1. Preheat air fryer to 360 degrees.
2. Pierce the sausage skin with a fork.
3. Put the sausage in the air fryer and cook for 12 to 15 minutes. After about 6 minutes, give the fryer tray a good shake to prevent overcooking in any area.
4. Serve with eggs or cut up to use in another recipe.

Nutrition Info:

- Calories: 106 kcal Carbs: 10g Fat: 3.2g Protein: 9g

Fried Egg

Servings: 1 | Cooking Time: 4 Minutes

Ingredients:

- 1 egg, pastured
- 1/8 teaspoon salt
- 1/8 teaspoon cracked black pepper

Directions:

1. Take the fryer pan, grease it with olive oil and then crack the egg in it.
2. Switch on the air fryer, insert fryer pan, then shut with its lid, and set the fryer at 370 degrees F.
3. Set the frying time to 3 minutes, then when the air fryer beep, open its lid and check the egg; if egg needs more cooking, then air fryer it for another minute.
4. Transfer the egg to a serving plate, season with salt and black pepper and serve.

Nutrition Info:

- Calories: 90 CalCarbs: 0.6 gFat: 7 gProtein: 6.3 gFiber: 0 g

Stir-fried Broccoli Stalks

Servings: 2 | Cooking Time: 2 Minutes

Ingredients:

- 1 lb. broccoli stalks, sliced into thin rounds
- ½-teaspoon olive brine
- ½-teaspoon caper brine
- Pinch dried chilies
- ½-teaspoon ground coriander
- ½-teaspoon ground cumin
- 3 black olives
- 2 garlic cloves, crushed
- Juice of 1 lemon
- ½ silver rind lemon
- 2 sun-dried tomatoes
- ½ tablespoons capers
- 3 cups stock
- Pinch of salt
- Pinch of pepper

Directions:

1. Preheat the Air Fryer to 330 degrees F.
2. Combine garlic, onion, capers, chilies, olives, sun-dried tomatoes, olive and caper brines, cumin, coriander, lemon juice, lemon rind, and half the stock. Stir well.
3. Meanwhile, layer broccoli stalks in the Air fryer basket. Fry for 2 minutes.
4. Wait for the mixture to become syrupy before adding the cooked broccoli stalks. Pour remaining lemon juice and stock. Season with salt and pepper. Serve.

Nutrition Info:

- Calorie: 138 Carbohydrate: 0g Fat: 1g Protein: 19g Fiber: 0g

Bacon Bbq

Servings: 2 | Cooking Time: 8 Minutes

Ingredients:

- 13g dark brown sugar
- 5g chili powder
- 1g ground cumin
- 1g cayenne pepper
- 4 slices bacon, halved

Directions:

1. Mix seasonings until well combined.

2. Dip the bacon in the dressing until it is completely covered. Leave aside.
3. Adjust the air fryer to 160°C.
4. Place the bacon in the preheated air fryer
5. Select Bacon option and press Start/Pause. Serve.

Nutrition Info:
- Calories: 1124 kcal Fat: 72g Carbs: 59g Protein: 49g

Avocado Taco Fry

Servings: 12 Slices | Cooking Time: 20 Minutes

Ingredients:
- 1 peeled avocado, sliced
- 1 beaten egg
- 1/2 cup panko bread crumbs
- Salt
- Tortillas and toppings

Directions:
1. Using a bowl, add in the egg.
2. Using a separate bowl, set in the breadcrumbs.
3. Dip the avocado into the bowl with the beaten egg and coat with the breadcrumbs. Sprinkle the coated wedges with a bit of salt.
4. Arrange them in the cooking basket in a single layer.
5. Set the Air Fryer to 392 degrees and cook for 15 minutes. Shake the basket halfway through the cooking process.

Nutrition Info:
- Calorie: 140 kcal Carbs: 12g Fat: 8.8g Protein: 6g

Cinnamon And Cheese Pancake

Servings: 4 | Cooking Time: 20 Minutes

Ingredients:
- 2 eggs
- 2 cups reduced-fat cream cheese
- 1/2 tsp. cinnamon
- 1 pack Stevia

Directions:
1. Adjust the Air Fryer to 330ºF.
2. Mix the cream cheese, cinnamon, eggs, and stevia.
3. Pour 1/4 of the mixture into the Air fryer basket.
4. Cook for 2 minutes on all sides. Repeat the process with the remaining portion of the mixture. Serve.

Nutrition Info:
- Calories: 140 kcal Carbs: 5.4g Fat: 10.6g Protein: 22.7g

Cocotte Eggs

Servings: 1 | Cooking Time: 15 Minutes

Ingredients:
- 1 tbsp. olive oil soup
- 2 tbsp. crumbly ricotta
- 1 tbsp. parmesan cheese soup

- 1 slice of gorgonzola cheese
- 1 slice of Brie cheese
- 1 tbsp. cream soup
- 1 egg
- Nutmeg and salt to taste
- Butternut to taste

Directions:
1. Spread with olive oil in the bottom of a small glass refractory. Place the cheese in the bottom and season with nutmeg and salt. Add the cream.
2. Break the egg into a cup and gently add it to the refractory mixture.
3. Preheat the air fryer for the time of 5 minutes and the temperature at 200C. Put the refractory in the basket of the air fryer, set the time to 10 minutes, and press the power button. Remove and serve still hot.

Nutrition Info:
- Calories: 138 Cal Carbs: 3 g Fat: 33 g Protein: 7.4 g Fiber: 2.2 g

Broccoli Mash

Servings: 4 | Cooking Time: 20-30 Minutes

Ingredients:
- 20 oz. Broccoli florets
- 3 oz. Butter; melted
- 1 garlic clove; minced
- 4 tbsp. Basil; chopped.
- A drizzle of olive oil
- A pinch of salt and black pepper

Directions:
1. Take a bowl and mix the broccoli with the oil, salt and pepper, toss and transfer to your air fryer's basket.
2. Cook at 380°f for 20 minutes, cool the broccoli down and put it in a blender
3. Add the rest of the ingredients, pulse, divide the mash between plates and serve as a side dish.

Nutrition Info:
- Calories: 200 Fat: 14g Fiber: 3g Carbs: 6g Protein: 7g

Bagels

Servings: 6 | Cooking Time: 20 Minutes

Ingredients:
- 2 cups almond flour
- 2 cups shredded mozzarella cheese, low-fat
- 2 tablespoons butter, unsalted
- 1 1/2 teaspoon baking powder
- 1 teaspoon apple cider vinegar
- 1 egg, pastured
- For Egg Wash:
- 1 egg, pastured
- 1 teaspoon butter, unsalted, melted

Directions:

1. Place flour in a heatproof bowl, add cheese and butter, then stir well and microwave for 90 seconds until butter and cheese has melted.
2. Then stir the mixture until well combined, let it cool for 5 minutes and whisk in the egg, baking powder, and vinegar until incorporated and dough comes together.
3. Let the dough cool for 10 minutes, then divide the dough into six sections, shape each section into a bagel and let the bagels rest for 5 minutes.
4. Prepare the egg wash and for this, place the melted butter in a bowl, whisk in the egg until blended and then brush the mixture generously on top of each bagel.
5. Take a fryer basket, line it with parchment paper and then place prepared bagels in it in a single layer.
6. Switch on the air fryer, insert fryer, then shut with its lid, set the fryer at 350 degrees F and cook for 10 minutes at the 350 degrees F until bagels are nicely golden and thoroughly cooked, turning the bagels halfway through the frying.
7. When air fryer beeps, open its lid, transfer bagels to a serving plate and cook the remaining bagels in the same manner.
8. Serve straight away.

Nutrition Info:
• Calories: 408.7 CalCarbs: 8.3 gFat: 33.5 gProtein: 20.3 gFiber: 4 g

French Toast In Sticks

Servings: 4 | Cooking Time: 10 Minutes

Ingredients:
• 4 slices of white bread, 38 mm thick, preferably hard
• 2 eggs
• 60 ml of milk
• 15 ml maple sauce
• 2 ml vanilla extract
• Nonstick Spray Oil
• 38g of sugar
• 3ground cinnamon
• Maple syrup, to serve
• Sugar to sprinkle

Directions:
1. Cut each slice of bread into thirds making 12 pieces. Place sideways
2. Beat the eggs, milk, maple syrup and vanilla.
3. Preheat the air fryer, set it to 175°C.
4. Dip the sliced bread in the egg mixture and place it in the preheated air fryer. Sprinkle French toast generously with oil spray.
5. Cook French toast for 10 minutes at 175°C. Turn the toast halfway through cooking.
6. Mix the sugar and cinnamon in a bowl.
7. Cover the French toast with the sugar and cinnamon mixture when you have finished cooking.
8. Serve with Maple syrup and sprinkle with powdered sugar

Nutrition Info:
• Calories 128 Fat 6.2 g, Carbohydrates 16.3 g, Sugar 3.3 g, Protein 3.2 g, Cholesterol 17 mg

Baked Eggs

Servings: 2 | Cooking Time: 17 Minutes

Ingredients:
• 2 tablespoons frozen spinach, thawed
• ½ teaspoon salt
• ¼ teaspoon ground black pepper
• 2 eggs, pastured
• 3 teaspoons grated parmesan cheese, reduced-fat
• 2 tablespoons milk, unsweetened, reduced-fat

Directions:
1. Switch on the air fryer, insert fryer basket, grease it with olive oil, then shut with its lid, set the fryer at 330 degrees F and preheat for 5 minutes.
2. Meanwhile, take two silicon muffin cups, grease them with oil, then crack an egg into each cup and evenly add cheese, spinach, and milk.
3. Season the egg with salt and black pepper and gently stir the ingredients, without breaking the egg yolk.
4. Open the fryer, add muffin cups in it, close with its lid and cook for 8 to 12 minutes until eggs have cooked to desired doneness.
5. When air fryer beeps, open its lid, take out the muffin cups and serve.

Nutrition Info:
• Calories: 161 CalCarbs: 3 gFat: 11.4 gProtein: 12.1 gFiber: 1.1 g

Garlic Bread

Servings: 5 | Cooking Time: 15 Minutes

Ingredients:
• 2 stale French rolls
• 4 tbsps. Crushed or crumpled garlic
• 1 cup mayonnaise
• Powdered grated Parmesan
• 1 tbsp. olive oil

Directions:
1. Preheat the air fryer to 200ºC for 5 minutes.
2. Mix mayonnaise with garlic and set aside.
3. Cut the baguettes into slices, but without separating them completely.
4. Fill the cavities of equals, then brush with olive oil and sprinkle with grated cheese.
5. Place in the basket of the air fryer. Cook for 10 minutes at 180ºC. Serve.

Nutrition Info:
• Calories: 151 kcal Fat: 7.1g Carbs: 17.9g Protein: 3.6g

Breakfast Pizza

Servings: 1-2 | Cooking Time: 8 Minutes

Ingredients:

- 10 ml of olive oil
- 1 prefabricated pizza dough (178 mm)
- 28g low moisture mozzarella cheese
- 2 slices smoked ham
- 1 egg
- 2g chopped cilantro

Directions:

1. Pass olive oil over the prefabricated pizza dough.
2. Add mozzarella cheese and smoked ham in the dough.
3. Preheat the air fryer, set it to 175°C.
4. Place the pizza in the preheated air fryer and cook for 8 minutes at 175°C.
5. Remove the baskets after 5 minutes and open the egg on the pizza.
6. Replace the baskets in the air fryer and finish cooking. Garnish with chopped coriander and serve.

Nutrition Info:

- Calories: 224 Fat: 7.5g Carbohydrates: 25.2g Protein: 14g Sugar: 0g Cholesterol: 13mg

Stuffed French Toast

Servings: 1 | Cooking Time: 10 Minutes

Ingredients:

- 1 slice of brioche bread,
- 64 mm thick, preferably rancid
- 113g cream cheese
- 2 eggs
- 15 ml of milk
- 30 ml whipping cream
- 38g of sugar
- 3g cinnamon
- 2 ml vanilla extract
- Nonstick Spray Oil
- Pistachios chopped to cover
- Maple syrup, to serve

Directions:

1. Preheat the air fryer, set it to 175°C.
2. Cut a slit in the middle of the muffin.
3. Fill the inside of the slit with cream cheese. Leave aside.
4. Mix the eggs, milk, whipping cream, sugar, cinnamon, and vanilla extract.
5. Moisten the stuffed French toast in the egg mixture for 10 seconds on each side.
6. Sprinkle each side of French toast with oil spray.
7. Place the French toast in the preheated air fryer and cook for 10 minutes at 175°C
8. Stir the French toast carefully with a spatula when you finish cooking.
9. Serve topped with chopped pistachios and acrid syrup.

Nutrition Info:

- Calories: 159 Fat: 7.5g Carbohydrates: 25.2g Protein: 14g Sugar: 0g Cholesterol:90mg

Cornbread

Servings: 8 | Cooking Time: 25 Minutes

Ingredients:

- 3/4 cup almond flour
- 1 cup white cornmeal
- 1 tablespoon erythritol sweetener
- 1 1/2 teaspoons baking powder
- 1/4 teaspoon salt
- 1/2 teaspoon baking soda
- 6 tablespoons butter, unsalted; melted
- 2 eggs; beaten
- 1 1/2 cups buttermilk, low-fat

Directions:

1. Switch on the air fryer, insert fryer pan, grease it with olive oil, then shut with its lid, set the fryer at 360 degrees F and preheat for 5 minutes.
2. Meanwhile, crack the egg in a bowl and then whisk in butter and milk until blended.
3. Place flour in another bowl, add remaining ingredients, stir until well mixed and then stir in egg mixture until incorporated.
4. Open the fryer, pour the batter into the fryer pan, close with its lid and cook for 25 minutes at the 360 degrees F until nicely golden and crispy, shaking halfway through the frying.
5. When air fryer beeps, open its lid, take out the fryer pan, and then transfer the bread onto a serving plate.
6. Cut the bread into pieces and serve.

Nutrition Info:

- Calories: 138 CalCarbs: 25 gFat: 2 gProtein: 5 gFiber: 2 g

Cauliflower Potato Mash

Servings: 4 | Cooking Time: 30 Minutes

Ingredients:

- 2 cups potatoes, peeled and cubed
- 2 tbsp. butter
- ¼ cup milk
- 10 oz. cauliflower florets
- ¾ tsp. salt

Directions:

1. Add water to the saucepan and bring to boil.
2. Reduce heat and simmer for 10 minutes.
3. Drain vegetables well. Transfer vegetables, butter, milk, and salt in a blender and blend until smooth.
4. Serve and enjoy.

Nutrition Info:

- Calories 128 Fat 6.2 g, Carbohydrates 16.3 g, Sugar 3.3 g, Protein 3.2 g, Cholesterol 17 mg

Spinach And Tomato Frittata

Servings: 4 | Cooking Time: 21 Minutes

Ingredients:

- 4 tablespoons chopped spinach
- 4 mushrooms, sliced
- 3 cherry tomatoes, halved
- 1 green onion, sliced
- 1 tablespoon chopped parsley
- ¾ teaspoon salt
- 1 tablespoon chopped rosemary
- 4 eggs, pastured
- 3 tablespoons heavy cream, reduced-fat
- 4 tablespoons grated cheddar cheese, reduced-fat

Directions:

1. Switch on the air fryer, insert fryer pan, grease it with olive oil, then shut with its lid, set the fryer at 350 degrees F and preheat for 5 minutes.
2. Meanwhile, crack eggs in a bowl, whisk in the cream until smooth, then add remaining ingredients and stir until well combined.
3. Then open the fryer, pour the frittata mixture in it, close with its lid and cook for 12 to 16 minutes until its top is nicely golden, frittata has set, and inserted toothpick into the frittata slides out clean.
4. When air fryer beeps, open its lid, transfer frittata onto a serving plate, then cut into pieces and serve.

Nutrition Info:

- Calories: 147 CalCarbs: 3 gFat: 11 gProtein: 9 gFiber: 1 g

Muffins Sandwich

Servings: 1 | Cooking Time: 10 Minutes

Ingredients:

- Nonstick Spray Oil
- 1 slice of white cheddar cheese
- 1 slice of Canadian bacon
- 1 English muffin, divided
- 15 ml hot water
- 1 large egg
- Salt and pepper to taste

Directions:

1. Spray the inside of an 85g mold with oil spray and place it in the air fryer.
2. Preheat the air fryer, set it to 160°C.
3. Add the Canadian cheese and bacon in the preheated air fryer.
4. Pour the hot water and the egg into the hot pan and season with salt and pepper.
5. Select Bread, set to 10 minutes.
6. Take out the English muffins after 7 minutes, leaving the egg for the full time.
7. Build your sandwich by placing the cooked egg on top of the English muffing and serve

Nutrition Info:

- Calories 400 Fat 26g, Carbohydrates 26g, Sugar 15 g, Protein 3 g, Cholesterol 155 mg

Zucchini And Walnut Cake With Maple Flavor Icing

Servings: 5 | Cooking Time: 35 Minutes

Ingredients:

- 1 9-ounce package of yellow cake mix
- 1 egg
- ⅓ cup of water
- ½ cup grated zucchini
- ¼ cup chopped walnuts
- ¾ tsp. of cinnamon
- ¼ tsp. nutmeg
- ¼ tsp. ground ginger
- Maple Flavor Glaze

Directions:

1. Preheat the fryer to a temperature of 350°F. Prepare an 8 x 3⅞ inch loaf pan. Prepare the cake dough according to package directions, using ⅓ cup of water instead of ½ cup. Add zucchini, nuts, cinnamon, nutmeg, and ginger.
2. Pour the dough into the prepared mold and put it inside the basket. Bake until a toothpick inserted in the middle of the cake is clean when removed for 32 to 34 minutes.
3. Remove the cake from the fryer and let it cool on a grill for 10 minutes. Then, remove the cake and place it on a serving plate. Stop cooling just warm. Spray it with maple flavor glaze.

Nutrition Info:

- Calories: 196 Carbohydrates: 27gFat: 11g Protein: 1g Sugar: 7g Cholesterol: 0mg

Tasty Chicken Patties

Servings: 4 | Cooking Time: 5 Minutes

Ingredients:

- 1 lb ground chicken
- 1/4 tsp red pepper flakes
- 1/2 tsp chili seasoning, no salt added
- 1/2 tsp ground cumin
- 1 tsp. paprika

Directions:

1. Preheat the air fryer grill.
2. Add all ingredients into the large bowl and mix well to combine.
3. Make four small round patties from the mixture.
4. Once the air fryer grill is hot, then place patties and grill for 5 minutes on each side.
5. Serve and enjoy.

Nutrition Info:

- Calories 220 Fat 8.6 g Carbohydrates 0.8 g Sugar 0.1 g Protein 33 g Cholesterol 101 mg

Roasted Broccoli

Servings: 2 | Cooking Time: 20-30 Minutes

Ingredients:

- 4 slices sugar-free bacon; cooked and crumbled
- 1 scallion, sliced on the bias.
- ¼ cup full-fat sour cream.
- 3 cups fresh broccoli florets.
- ½ cup shredded sharp cheddar cheese.
- 1 tbsp. Coconut oil

Directions:

1. Place broccoli into the air fryer basket and drizzle it with coconut oil.
2. Adjust the temperature to 350 degrees f and set the timer for 10 minutes.
3. Toss the basket two- or three-times during cooking to avoid burned spots
4. When broccoli begins to crisp at ends, remove from fryer.
5. Top with shredded cheese, sour cream and crumbled bacon and garnish with scallion slices.

Nutrition Info:

- Calories: 361 Protein: 18.4g Fiber: 3.6g Fat: 25.7g Carbs: 10.5g

Scallion Sandwich

Servings: 1 | Cooking Time: 15 Minutes

Ingredients:

- 2 slices wheat bread
- 2 tsps. Low-fat butter
- 2 sliced scallions
- 1 tbsp. grated parmesan cheese
- 3/4 cup low-fat, grated cheddar cheese

Directions:

1. Adjust the Air fryer to 356ºF.
2. Apply butter to a slice of bread.
3. Then place it inside the cooking air fryer basket with the butter side facing down.
4. Place cheese and scallions on top. Spread the rest of the butter on the other slice of bread. Then put it on top of the sandwich.
5. Allow to cook for 10 minutes. Serve.

Nutrition Info:

- Calories: 154 kcal Carbs: 9g Fat: 2.5g Protein: 8.6g

Breakfast Muffins

Servings: 2 | Cooking Time: 6 Minutes

Ingredients:

- 2 whole-wheat English muffins
- 4 slices bacon
- Pepper
- 2 eggs

Directions:

1. Crack an egg each into ramekins then season with pepper.
2. Place the ramekins and bacon in your preheated air fryer at 390˚F.
3. Allow to cook for 6-minutes with the bacon and muffins.
4. When the bacon and eggs are done cooking, add two pieces of bacon and one egg to each egg muffin. Serve when hot.

Nutrition Info:

- Calories: 276 kcal Total Fat: 12g Carbs: 10.2g Protein: 17.3g

Shrimp And Black Bean Salad

Servings: 6 | Cooking Time: None

Ingredients:

- ¼ cup apple cider vinegar
- 3 tablespoons olive oil
- 1 teaspoon ground cumin
- ½ teaspoon chipotle chili powder
- ¼ teaspoon salt
- 1 pound cooked shrimp, peeled and deveined
- 1 (15-ounce) can black beans, rinsed and drained
- 1 cup diced tomatoes
- 1 small green pepper, diced
- ¼ cup sliced green onions
- ¼ cup fresh chopped cilantro

Directions:

1. Whisk together the vinegar, olive oil, cumin, chili powder, and salt in a large bowl.
2. Chop the shrimp into bite-sized pieces then add to the bowl.
3. Toss in the beans, tomatoes, bell pepper, green onion, and cilantro until well combined.
4. Cover until ready to serve.

Nutrition Info:

- Calories 375 Total Fat 15g Saturated Fat 3.1g Total Carbs 36.3g Net Carbs 28.2g Protein 26.2g Sugar 8.3g Fiber 8.1g Sodium 627mg

Air Fryer Scrambled Egg

Servings: 2 | Cooking Time: 10 Minutes

Ingredients:

- 2 eggs
- 1 chopped tomato
- Dash of salt
- 1 tsp. butter
- 1/4 cup cream

Directions:

1. Put the eggs in a bowl then add salt and the cream. Whisk until fluffy.
2. Adjust the air fryer to 300°F.
3. Add butter to baking pan and place it into the preheated air fryer.
4. Add the egg mixture to the baking pan once the butter has melted.
5. Cook for 10-minutes. Serve warm.

Nutrition Info:

- Calories: 105 kcal Carbs: 2.3g Fat: 8g Protein: 6.4g

Peanut Butter & Banana Breakfast Sandwich

Servings: 1 | Cooking Time: 6 Minutes

Ingredients:

- 2 slices whole-wheat bread
- 1 tsp. sugar-free maple syrup
- 1 sliced banana
- 2 tbsps. Peanut butter

Directions:

1. Evenly coat each side of the sliced bread with peanut butter.
2. Add the sliced banana and drizzle with some sugar-free maple syrup.
3. Adjust the air fryer to 330°F then cook for 6 minutes. Serve warm.

Nutrition Info:

- Calories: 211 kcal Total Fat: 8.2g Carbs: 6.3g Protein: 11.2g

Tortilla

Servings: Two | Cooking Time: 20 Minutes

Ingredients:

- 2 eggs
- 2 slices of ham, chopped
- 2 slices of chopped mozzarella
- 1 tbsp. chopped onion soup
- ½ cup chopped parsley and chives tea
- Salt, black pepper and oregano to taste
- Olive oil spread

Directions:

1. Preheat the air fryer for the time of 5 minutes and the temperature at 200C.
2. Spread a refractory that fits in the basket of the air fryer and has a high shelf and reserve.
3. In a bowl, beat the eggs lightly with a fork. Add the fillings and spices. Place the refractory container in the basket of the air fryer and pour the beaten eggs being careful not to fall.
4. Set the time from 10 to 15 minutes and press the power button. The tortilla is ready when it is golden brown

Nutrition Info:

- Calories: 41 Fat: 1.01g Carbohydrates: 6.68g Protein: 1.08g Sugar: 0.25g Cholesterol: 0mg

Herb Frittata

Servings: 4 | Cooking Time: 25 Minutes

Ingredients:

- 2 tablespoons chopped green scallions
- 1/2 teaspoon ground black pepper
- 2 tablespoons chopped cilantro
- 1/2 teaspoon salt
- 2 tablespoons chopped parsley
- 1/2 cup half and half, reduced-fat
- 4 eggs, pastured
- 1/3 cup shredded cheddar cheese, reduced-fat

Directions:

1. Switch on the air fryer, insert fryer basket, grease it with olive oil, then shut with its lid, set the fryer at 330 degrees F and preheat for 10 minutes.
2. Meanwhile, take a round heatproof pan that fits into the fryer basket, grease it well with oil and set aside until required.
3. Crack the eggs in a bowl, beat in half-and-half, then add remaining ingredients, beat until well mixed and pour the mixture into prepared pan.
4. Open the fryer, place the pan in it, close with its lid and cook for 15 minutes at the 330 degrees F until its top is nicely golden, frittata has set and inserted toothpick into the frittata slides out clean.
5. When air fryer beeps, open its lid, take out the pan, then transfer frittata onto a serving plate, cut it into pieces and serve.

Nutrition Info:

- Calories: 141 CalCarbs: 2 gFat: 10 gProtein: 8 gFiber: 0 g

Lean Lamb And Turkey Meatballs With Yogurt

Servings: 4

Ingredients:

- 1 egg white
- 4 ounces ground lean turkey
- 1 pound of ground lean lamb
- 1 teaspoon each of cayenne pepper, ground coriander, red chili paste, salt, and ground cumin
- 2 garlic cloves, minced
- 1 1/2 tablespoons parsley, chopped
- 1 tablespoon mint, chopped
- 1/4 cup of olive oil
- For the yogurt
- 2 tablespoons of buttermilk
- 1 garlic clove, minced
- 1/4 cup mint, chopped
- 1/2 cup of Greek yogurt, non-fat
- Salt to taste

Directions:

1. Set the Air Fryer to 390 degrees.
2. Mix all the ingredients for the meatballs in a bowl. Roll and mold them into golf-size round pieces. Arrange in the cooking basket. Cook for 8 minutes.
3. While waiting, combine all the ingredients for the mint yogurt in a bowl. Mix well.
4. Serve the meatballs with the mint yogurt. Top with olives and fresh mint.

Nutrition Info:

- Calorie: 154 Carbohydrate: 9g Fat: 2.5g Protein: 8.6g Fiber: 2.4g

Breakfast Cheese Bread Cups

Servings: 2 | Cooking Time: 15 Minutes

Ingredients:

- 2 eggs
- 2 tbsps. Grated cheddar cheese
- Salt and pepper
- 1 ham slice cut into 2 pieces
- 4 bread slices flatted with a rolling pin

Directions:

1. Spray both sides of the ramekins with cooking spray.
2. Place two slices of bread into each ramekin.
3. Add the ham slice pieces into each ramekin. Crack an egg in each ramekin then sprinkle with cheese. Season with salt and pepper.
4. Place the ramekins into air fryer at 300°Fahrenheit for 15-minutes.
5. Serve warm.

Nutrition Info:

- Calories: 162 kcal Total Fat: 8g Carbs: 10g Protein: 11g

Chickpea, Tuna, And Kale Salad

Servings: 1 | Cooking Time: None

Ingredients:

- 2 ounces fresh kale
- 2 tablespoons fat-free honey mustard dressing
- 1 (3-ounce) pouch tuna in water, drained
- 1 medium carrot, shredded
- Salt and pepper

Directions:

1. Trim the thick stems from the kale and cut into bite-sized pieces.
2. Toss the kale with the dressing in a salad bowl.
3. Top with tuna, chickpeas, and carrots. Season with salt and pepper to serve.

Nutrition Info:

- Calories 215 Total Fat 0.6g Saturated Fat 0g Total Carbs 28.1g Net Carbs 23.6g Protein 22.5g Sugar 16g Fiber 4.5g Sodium 1176mg

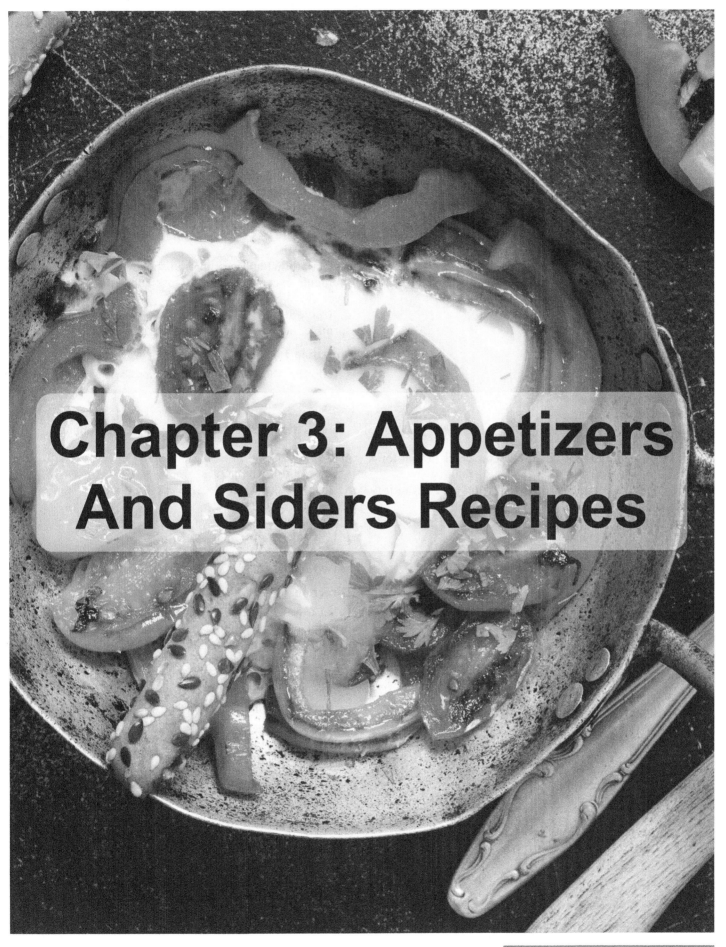

Chapter 3: Appetizers And Siders Recipes

Chapter 3: Appetizers And Siders Recipes

Chicken Croquette

Servings: 4 | Cooking Time: 15 Minutes

Ingredients:

- 2- lb. boneless chicken
- 1st Marinade:
- 3- tbsp. vinegar or lemon juice
- 2 or 3 tsp. paprika
- 1 tsp. black pepper
- 1 tsp. salt
- 3 tsp. ginger-garlic paste
- 2nd Marinade:
- 1 cup yogurt
- 4- tsp. tandoori masala
- 2- tbsp. dry fenugreek leaves
- 1 tsp. black salt
- 1 tsp. chat masala
- 1 tsp. garam masala powder
- 1 tsp. red chili powder
- 1 tsp. salt
- 3- drops of red color

Directions:

1. Make the 1st marinade and drench the chicken in it for 4 hours.
2. Make the 2nd marinade and sprinkle the chicken in it to let the flavors blend.
3. Preheat the Air Fryer to 160 F and cook for 15 minutes.
4. Serve with mint chutney.

Nutrition Info:

- Calories: 73 Protein: 1.1g Fiber: 1.1g Fat: 6.5g Carbs: 3.3g

Air Fryer Mini Pizza

Servings: 1 | Cooking Time:5 Minutes

Ingredients:

- Sliced olives: 1/4 cup
- One pita bread
- One tomato
- Shredded cheese: 1/2 cup

Directions:

1. Let the air fryer preheat to 350 F
2. Lay pita flat on a plate. Add cheese, slices of tomatoes, and olives.
3. Cook for five minutes at 350 F
4. Take the pizza out of the air fryer.
5. Slice it and enjoy

Nutrition Info:

- Calories: 344kcal | Carbohydrates: 37g | Protein: 18g | Fat: 13g |

Herbed Radish Sauté

Servings: 4 | Cooking Time: 15 Minutes

Ingredients:

- 2 bunches red radishes; halved
- 2 tbsp. parsley; chopped.
- 2 tbsp. balsamic vinegar
- 1 tbsp. olive oil
- Salt and black pepper to taste

Directions:

1. Get a bowl and mix the radishes with the remaining ingredients except the parsley, toss and put them in your air fryer's basket.
2. Cook at 400°F for 15 minutes, divide between plates, sprinkle the parsley on top and serve as a side dish.

Nutrition Info:

- Calories: 180 Fat: 4g Fiber: 2g Carbs: 3g Protein: 5g

Avocado Egg Rolls

Servings: 10 | Cooking Time: 15 Minutes

Ingredients:

- Ten egg roll wrappers
- Diced sundried tomatoes: ¼ cup oil drained
- Avocados, cut in cube
- Red onion: 2/3 cup chopped
- 1/3 cup chopped cilantro
- Kosher salt and freshly ground black pepper
- Two small limes: juice

Directions:

1. In a bowl, add sundried tomatoes, avocado, cilantro, lime juice, pepper, onion, and kosher salt mix well gently.
2. Lay egg roll wrapper flat on a surface, add ¼ cup of filling in the wrapper's bottom.
3. Seal with water and make it into a roll.
4. Spray the rolls with olive oil.
5. Cook at 400 F in the air fryer for six minutes. Turn halfway through.
6. Serve with dipping sauce.

Nutrition Info:

- 160 Cal| total fat 19g |carbohydrates 5.6g |protein 19.2g

Pop Tarts

Servings: 4 | Cooking Time: 7 Minutes

Ingredients:

- 1 homemade pie crust, rolled out
- 1/2 cup strawberry jam
- Cooking spray
- 1/2 cup Greek yogurt

Directions:

1. Set pie crust in place.
2. Slice out two shapes for every pop tart you wish to prepare. Take 1 tbsp. jam and spread to the edges.
3. Set the other cutout on top of the jam and press the edges gently together. Set in your air fryer.
4. Top the tarts with sprinkles of cooking spray.
5. Allow to cook at 370ºF for 10 minutes.
6. Top with yogurt.
7. Enjoy.

Nutrition Info:

- Calories: 190 kcal; Fat: 4.5g; Carbs: 35g; Proteins: 2g

Air Fryer Roasted Bananas

Servings: 1 | Cooking Time: 8 Minutes

Ingredients:

- 1 banana, sliced into 1/8-inch pieces
- Avocado oil

Directions:

1. Set a parchment paper to your air fryer basket.
2. Set the banana pieces on the basket and avoid overlapping. You can cook in batches if need be. Sprinkle avocado oil to the slices.
3. Set in the air fryer and allow to cook for 5 minutes at 375F. You can add 3 extra minutes to ensure they are browned and caramelized.

Nutrition Info:

- Calories: 107 kcal; Carbs: 27g; Proteins: 1.3g; Fat: 0.7g

Roasted Eggplant

Servings: 4 | Cooking Time: 30 Minutes

Ingredients:

- 1 large eggplant
- tbsps. Olive oil
- 1/2 tsp. Garlic powder.
- Salt

Directions:

1. Remove top and bottom from the eggplant. Slice eggplant into 1/4-inch-thick round slices.
2. Brush slices with olive oil. Sprinkle with salt and garlic powder
3. Place eggplant slices into the air fryer basket. Adjust the temperature to 390ºF and set the timer for 15 minutes.

Serve immediately.

Nutrition Info:

- Calories: 91 kcal; Protein: 1.3g; Fat: 6.7g; Carbs: 7.5g

Cabbage And Radishes Mix

Servings: 4 | Cooking Time: 15 Minutes

Ingredients:

- 6 cups green cabbage; shredded
- ½ cup celery leaves; chopped.
- ¼ cup green onions; chopped.
- 6 radishes; sliced
- 3 tbsp. olive oil
- 2 tbsp. balsamic vinegar
- ½ tsp. hot paprika
- 1 tsp. lemon juice

Directions:

1. In your air fryer's pan, combine all the ingredients and toss well.
2. Take out the pan in the fryer and cook at 380°F for 15 minutes. Divide between plates and serve as a side dish

Nutrition Info:

- Calories: 130 Fat: 4g Fiber: 3g Carbs: 4g Protein: 7g

Cheesy Bell Pepper Eggs

Servings:4 | Cooking Time: 15 Min

Ingredients:

- 4 medium green bell peppers
- 3 ounces cooked ham, chopped
- 1/4 medium onion, peeled and chopped
- 8 large eggs
- 1 cup mild Cheddar cheese

Directions:

1. Cut each bell pepper from its tops. Pick the seeds with a small knife and the white membranes. Place onion and ham into each pepper.
2. Break two eggs into each chili pepper. Cover with 1/4 cup of peppered cheese. Put the basket into the air fryer.
3. Set the temperature to 390 ° F and change the timer for 15 minutes.
4. Peppers will be tender when fully fried, and the eggs will be solid. Serve hot.

Nutrition Info:

- calories: 314| protein: 24.9g| fiber: 1.7g| net carbohydrates: 4.6g fat: 18.6g| carbohydrates: 6.3g|

Creamy Fennel

Servings: 4 | Cooking Time: 12 Minutes

Ingredients:

- 2 big fennel bulbs; sliced
- ½ cup coconut cream
- 2 tbsp. butter; melted
- Salt and black pepper to taste.

Directions:

1. In a pan that fits the air fryer, combine all the ingredients, toss, introduce in the machine and cook at 370°F for 12 minutes
2. Divide between plates and serve as a side dish.

Nutrition Info:

- Calories: 151 Fat: 3g Fiber: 2g Carbs: 4g Protein: 6g

Garlic & Cheese Potatoes

Servings: 4 | Cooking Time: 40 Minutes

Ingredients:

- halved Idaho baking potatoes
- 1 tbsp. garlic powder
- Salt
- ½ cup shredded cheddar cheese
- 1 tsp. parsley

Directions:

1. Toss all your ingredients in a bowl except cheese.
2. Place potatoes in a baking dish and sprinkle cheese over top of them.
3. Set in the air fryers and cook for 40 minutes at 390°F.

Nutrition Info:

- Calories: 498 kcal; Fat: 19.09g; Carbs: 67.27g; Protein: 16.5g

Honey Chili Chicken

Servings: 3 | Cooking Time: 15 Minutes

Ingredients:

- For chicken fingers:
- 1 lb. chicken
- 2 ½- tsp. ginger-garlic paste
- 1 tsp. red chili sauce
- ¼- tsp. salt
- ¼- tsp. red chili powder
- Edible orange food coloring
- For sauce:
- 2 tbsp. olive oil
- 1 capsicum
- 2 small onions
- 1 ½- tsp. ginger garlic paste
- ½- tbsp. red chili sauce
- 2 tbsp. tomato ketchup
- 1 ½- tbsp. sweet chili sauce
- 2 tsp. soy sauce

- 2 tsp. vinegar
- 1-2 tbsp. honey
- A pinch of black pepper
- 2 tsp. red chili flakes

Directions:

1. Blend all of the components for the marinade and marinate veal fingers for 30 minutes.
2. Blend the breadcrumbs, oregano and red chili flakes and add the marinated fingers on this mix.
3. Preheat the Air Fryer to 160 F and cook for 15 minutes, shaking the fry basket occasionally.

Nutrition Info:

- Calories 295 Fat 17 g Carbohydrates 4 g Sugar 0.1 g Protein 29 g Cholesterol 260 mg

Green Beans

Servings: 4 | Cooking Time: 20 Minutes

Ingredients:

- 6 cups green beans; trimmed
- 1 tbsp. hot paprika
- 2 tbsp. olive oil
- A pinch of salt and black pepper

Directions:

1. Get a bowl and mix the green beans with the other ingredients, toss, put them in the air fryer's basket and cook at 370°F for 20 minutes
2. Divide between plates and serve as a side dish.

Nutrition Info:

- Calories: 120 Fat: 5g Fiber: 1g Carbs: 4g Protein: 2g

Ravioli

Servings: 4 | Cooking Time: 16 Minutes

Ingredients:

- 8 ounces frozen vegan ravioli, thawed
- 1 teaspoon dried basil
- 1 teaspoon garlic powder
- 1/8 teaspoon ground black pepper
- ¼ teaspoon salt
- 1 teaspoon dried oregano
- 2 teaspoons nutritional yeast flakes
- 1/2 cup marinara sauce, unsweetened
- 1/2 cup panko bread crumbs
- 1/4 cup liquid from chickpeas can

Directions:

1. Place breadcrumbs in a bowl, sprinkle with salt, basil, oregano, and black pepper, add garlic powder and yeast and stir until mixed.
2. Take a bowl and then pour in chickpeas liquid in it.
3. Working on one ravioli at a time, first dip a ravioli in chickpeas liquid and then coat with breadcrumbs mixture.
4. Prepare remaining ravioli in the same manner, then take

a fryer basket, grease it well with oil and place ravioli in it in a single layer.

5. Switch on the air fryer, insert fryer basket, sprinkle oil on ravioli, shut with its lid, set the fryer at 390 degrees F, then cook for 6 minutes, turn the ravioli and continue cooking 2 minutes until nicely golden and heated thoroughly.

6. Cook the remaining ravioli in the same manner and serve with marinara sauce.

Nutrition Info:

• Calories: 150 CalCarbs: 27 gFat: 3 gProtein: 5 gFiber: 2 g

Air Fryer Onion Rings

Servings: 4 | Cooking Time:10 Minutes

Ingredients:

• 1 egg whisked
• One large onion
• Whole-wheat breadcrumbs: 1 and 1/2 cup
• Smoked paprika: 1 teaspoon
• Flour: 1 cup
• Garlic powder: 1 teaspoon
• Buttermilk: 1 cup
• Kosher salt and pepper to taste

Directions:

1. Cut the stems of the onion. Then cut into half-inch-thick rounds.

2. In a bowl, add flour, pepper, garlic powder, smoked paprika, and salt. Then add egg and buttermilk. Mix to combine.

3. In another bowl, add the breadcrumbs.

4. Coat the onions in buttermilk mix, then in breadcrumbs mix.

5. Freeze these breaded onions for 15 minutes. Spray the fryer basket with oil spray.

6. Put onions in the air fryer basket in one single layer. Spray the onion with cooking oil.

7. Cook at 370 degrees for 10-12 minutes. Flip only, if necessary.

8. Serve with sauce.

Nutrition Info:

• 205 Kcal |total fat 5.5g |carbohydrates 7.5g | protein 18g

Air Fryer Buffalo Cauliflower

Servings: 4 | Cooking Time:15 Minutes

Ingredients:

• Homemade buffalo sauce: 1/2 cup
• One head of cauliflower, cut bite-size pieces
• Butter melted: 1 tablespoon
• Olive oil
• Kosher salt & pepper, to taste

Directions:

1. Spray cooking oil on the air fryer basket.

2. In a bowl, add buffalo sauce, melted butter, pepper, and salt. Mix well.

3. Put the cauliflower bits in the air fryer and spray the olive oil over it. Let it cook at 400 F for 7 minutes.

4. Remove the cauliflower from the air fryer and add it to the sauce. Coat the cauliflower well.

5. Put the sauce coated cauliflower back into the air fryer.

6. Cook at 400 F, for 7-8 minutes or until crispy.

7. Take out from the air fryer and serve with dipping sauce.

Nutrition Info:

• Calories 101kcal | Carbohydrates 4g | Protein 3g | Fat: 7g

Air Fryer Delicata Squash

Servings: 2 | Cooking Time:10 Minutes

Ingredients:

• Olive oil: 1/2 Tablespoon
• One delicata squash
• Salt: 1/2 teaspoon
• Rosemary: 1/2 teaspoon

Directions:

1. Chop the squash in slices of 1/4 thickness. Discard the seeds.

2. In a bowl, add olive oil, salt, rosemary with squash slices. Mix well.

3. Cook the squash for ten minutes at 400 F. flip the squash halfway through.

4. Make sure it is cooked completely.

5. Serve hot.

Nutrition Info:

• Cal: 69|Fat: 4g| Carbs: 9g|Protein 1g

Cauliflower Fritters

Servings: 2 | Cooking Time: 14 Minutes

Ingredients:

• 5 cups chopped cauliflower florets
• 1/2 cup almond flour
• 1/2 teaspoon baking powder
• ½ teaspoon ground black pepper
• ½ teaspoon salt
• 2 eggs, pastured

Directions:

1. Add chopped cauliflower in a blender or food processor, pulse until minced and then tip the mixture in a bowl.

2. Add remaining ingredients, stir well and then shape the mixture into 1/3-inch patties, an ice cream scoop of mixture per patty.

3. Switch on the air fryer, insert fryer basket, grease it with olive oil, then shut with its lid, set the fryer at 390 degrees F and preheat for 5 minutes.

4. Then open the fryer, add cauliflower patties in it in a single layer, spray oil over patties, close with its lid and cook for 14 minutes at the 375 degrees F until nicely golden and cooked, flipping the patties halfway through the frying.

5. Serve straight away with the dip.

Nutrition Info:
- Calories: 272 CalCarbs: 57 gFat: 0.3 gProtein: 11 gFiber: 8 g

Breakfast Bombs

Servings: 3 | Cooking Time: 15 Minutes

Ingredients:
- Three eggs (large), lightly whisked
- Less-fat cream cheese: two tbsp. Softened
- Chopped chives: 1 tablespoon fresh
- Freshly prepared whole-wheat pizza dough: 1/4 cup or 4 ounces
- Cooking spray
- 3 pieces of bacon: center cut
- Freshly prepared whole-wheat pizza dough: 1/4 cup or 4 ounces
- Cooking spray

Directions:
1. In a skillet, cook the bacon slices for about ten minutes. Crumble the cooked bacon. Add the eggs to the skillet and cook until loose for almost one minute. In another bowl, mix with chives, cheese, and bacon.
2. Cut the dough into four pieces. Make it into a five-inch circle.
3. Add 1/4 of egg mixture in the center of dough circle pieces.
4. Seal the dough seams with water and pinch
5. Add dough pockets in one single layer in the air fryer. Spray with cooking oil
6. Cook for 5-6 minutes, at 350°F or until light golden brown.
7. Serve hot.

Nutrition Info:
- Calories 305| Fat 15g| Protein 19g| Carbohydrate 26g|Fiber 2g

Air Fryer Roasted Corn

Servings: 4 | Cooking Time:10 Minutes

Ingredients:
- 4 corn ears
- Olive oil: 2 to 3 teaspoons
- Kosher salt and pepper to taste

Directions:
1. Clean the corn, wash, and pat dry.
2. Fit in the basket of air fryer, cut if need to.
3. Top with olive oil, kosher salt, and pepper.
4. Cook for ten minutes at 400 F.
5. Enjoy crispy roasted corn.

Nutrition Info:
- Kcal 28|Fat 2g|Net carbs 0 g |Protein 7 g

Air Fryer Crisp Egg Cups

Servings: 4 | Cooking Time: 10 Minutes

Ingredients:
- Toasted bread: 4 slices (whole-wheat)
- Cooking spray, nonstick
- Large eggs: 4
- Margarine: 1 and a half tbsp. (trans-fat free)
- Ham: 1 slice
- Salt: 1/8 tsp
- Black pepper: 1/8 tsp

Directions:
1. Let the air fryer Preheat to 375 F, with the air fryer basket.
2. Take four ramekins, spray with cooking spray.
3. Trim off the crusts from bread, add margarine to one side.
4. Put the bread down, into a ramekin, margarine-side in.
5. Press it in the cup. Cut the ham in strips, half-inch thick, and add on top of the bread.
6. Add one egg to the ramekins. Add salt and pepper.
7. Put the custard cups in the air fryer. Air fry at 375 F for 10–13 minutes.
8. Remove the ramekin from the air fryer and serve.

Nutrition Info:
- Calories 150|Total Fat 8g|Total Carbohydrate 6g Protein 12g

Keto French Fries

Servings: 4 | Cooking Time: 20 Minutes

Ingredients:
- 1 large rutabaga, peeled and cut into spears about ¼ inch wide.
- Salt and pepper
- 1/2 tsp. paprika
- 2 tbsps. coconut oil

Directions:
1. Preheat your air fryer to 450°F.
2. Mix the oil, paprika, salt, and pepper.
3. Pour the oil mixture over the fries, making sure all pieces are well coated.
4. Cook in the air fryer for 20 minutes or until crispy.

Nutrition Info:
- Calories: 113 kcal; Fat: 7.2g; Carbs: 12.5g; Protein: 1.9g

Kale & Celery Crackers

Servings: 6 | Cooking Time: 20 Min

Ingredients:
- One cups flax seed, ground
- 1 cups flax seed, soaked overnight and drained
- 2 bunches kale, chopped
- 1 bunch basil, chopped

- ½ bunch celery, chopped
- 2 garlic cloves, minced
- 1/3 cup olive oil

Directions:

1. Mix the ground flaxseed with the celery, kale, basil, and garlic in your food processor and mix well.
2. Add the oil and soaked flaxseed, then mix again, scatter in the pan of your air fryer, break into medium crackers and cook for 20 minutes at 380 degrees F.
3. Serve as an appetizer and break into cups.
4. Enjoy.

Nutrition Info:

- calories 143|fat 1g| fiber 2g| carbs 8g| Protein 4g

Vegetable Spring Rolls

Servings: 4 | Cooking Time: 15 Minutes

Ingredients:

- Toasted sesame seeds
- Large carrots – grated
- Spring roll wrappers
- One egg white
- Gluten-free soy sauce, a dash
- Half cabbage: sliced
- Olive oil: 2 tbsp.

Directions:

1. In a pan over high flame heat, 2 tbsp. of oil and sauté the chopped vegetables. Then add soy sauce. Do not overcook the vegetables.
2. Turn off the heat and add toasted sesame seeds.
3. Lay spring roll wrappers flat on a surface and add egg white with a brush on the sides.
4. Add some vegetable mix in the wrapper and fold.
5. Spray the spring rolls with oil spray and air dry for 8 minutes at 200 C.
6. Serve with dipping sauce.

Nutrition Info:

- 129 calories| fat 16.3g |carbohydrates 8.2g |protein 12.1 g

Chinese Chili

Servings: 4 | Cooking Time: 15 Minutes

Ingredients:

- For chicken fingers:
- 1 lb. chicken
- 2 ½- tsp. ginger-garlic paste
- 1 tsp. red chili sauce
- ¼- tsp. salt
- ¼- tsp. red chili powder/black pepper
- Edible orange food coloring
- For sauce:
- 2- tbsp. olive oil
- 1 ½- tsp. ginger garlic paste
- ½- tbsp. red chili sauce

- 2- tbsp. tomato ketchup
- 2- tsp. soy sauce
- 1-2- tbsp. honey
- ¼- tsp. Ajinomoto
- 1-2- tsp. red chili flakes

Directions:

1. Blend all of the components for the marinade and marinate chicken fingers for 30 minutes.
2. Blend the breadcrumbs, oregano and red chili flakes and add the marinated fingers on this mix.
3. Preheat the Air Fryer to 160 F and cook for 15 minutes, shaking the fry basket occasionally.

Nutrition Info:

- Calories 545 Fat 39.6 g Carbohydrates 9.5 g Sugar 3.1 g Protein 43 g Cholesterol 110 mg

Beef Steak Fingers

Servings: 4 | Cooking Time: 15 Minutes

Ingredients:

- 1 lb. boneless beef steak
- 2 cup dry breadcrumbs
- 2 tsp. oregano
- 2- tsp. red chili flakes
- Marinade:
- 1 ½- tbsp. ginger-garlic paste
- 4- tbsp. lemon juice
- 2- tsp. salt
- 1 tsp. pepper powder
- 1 tsp. red chili powder
- 6- tbsp. corn flour
- 4- eggs

Directions:

1. Blend all marinade ingredients and soak the meat for 20-30 minutes.
2. Blend the breadcrumbs, oregano and red chili well and dip the marinated fingers in this mix.
3. Preheat the Air Fryer to 160 F for 5 minutes. Cook for 15 minutes, shaking halfway through.

Nutrition Info:

- Calories 229 Fat 2.6 g Carbohydrates 10.9 g Sugar 6.1 g Protein 43.4 g Cholesterol 99 mg

Zucchini Fries

Servings: 4 | Cooking Time: 20 Minutes

Ingredients:

- 2 medium zucchinis
- ½ cup almond flour
- 1/8 teaspoon ground black pepper
- ½ teaspoon garlic powder
- 1/8 teaspoon salt
- 1 teaspoon Italian seasoning
- ½ cup grated parmesan cheese, reduced-fat

- 1 egg, pastured, beaten

Directions:

1. Switch on the air fryer, insert fryer basket, grease it with olive oil, then shut with its lid, set the fryer at 400 degrees F and preheat for 10 minutes.
2. Meanwhile, cut each zucchini in half and then cut each zucchini half into 4-inch-long pieces, each about ½-inch thick.
3. Place flour in a shallow dish, add remaining ingredients except for the egg and stir until mixed.
4. Crack the egg in a bowl and then whisk until blended.
5. Working on one zucchini piece at a time, first dip it in the egg, then coat it in the almond flour mixture and place it on a wire rack.
6. Open the fryer, add zucchini pieces in it in a single layer, spray oil over zucchini, close with its lid and cook for 10 minutes until nicely golden and crispy, shaking halfway through the frying.
7. Cook remaining zucchini pieces in the same manner and serve.

Nutrition Info:

- Calories: 147 CalCarbs: 6 gFat: 10 gProtein: 9 gFiber: 2 g

Curry Cabbage

Servings: 4 | Cooking Time: 30 Minutes

Ingredients:

- 30 oz. shredded Green cabbage
- tbsps. melted Coconut oil
- 1 tbsp. Red curry paste
- Salt and black pepper

Directions:

1. In a pan that fits the air fryer, combine the cabbage with the rest of the ingredients, toss, introduce the pan in the machine and cook at 380°F for 20 minutes
2. Divide between plates and serve as a side dish.

Nutrition Info:

- Calories: 180 kcal; Fat: 14g; Carbs: 6g; Protein: 8g

Avocado Fries

Servings: 2 | Cooking Time: 20 Minutes

Ingredients:

- 1 medium avocado, pitted
- 1 egg
- 1/2 cup almond flour
- ¼ teaspoon salt
- ¼ teaspoon ground black pepper
- 1/2 teaspoon salt

Directions:

1. Switch on the air fryer, insert fryer basket, grease it with olive oil, then shut with its lid, set the fryer at 400 degrees F and preheat for 10 minutes.

2. Meanwhile, cut the avocado in half and then cut each half into wedges, each about ½-inch thick.
3. Place flour in a shallow dish, add salt and black pepper and stir until mixed.
4. Crack the egg in a bowl and then whisk until blended.
5. Working on one avocado piece at a time, first dip it in the egg, then coat it in the almond flour mixture and place it on a wire rack.
6. Open the fryer, add avocado pieces in it in a single layer, spray oil over avocado, close with its lid and cook for 10 minutes until nicely golden and crispy, shaking halfway through the frying.
7. When air fryer beeps, open its lid, transfer avocado fries onto a serving plate and serve.

Nutrition Info:

- Calories: 251 CalCarbs: 19 gFat: 17 gProtein: 6 gFiber: 7 g

Veal Chili

Servings: 4 | Cooking Time: 15 Minutes

Ingredients:

- 1 lb. veal
- 2 ½- tsp. ginger-garlic paste
- 1 tsp. red chili sauce
- ¼- tsp. salt
- ¼- tsp. red chili powder/black pepper
- Edible orange food coloring
- For sauce:
- 2- tbsp. olive oil
- 1 ½- tsp. ginger garlic paste
- ½- tbsp. red chili sauce
- 2 -tbsp. tomato ketchup
- 2- tsp. soy sauce
- 1-2 tbsp. honey
- ¼- tsp. Ajinomoto
- 1-2 tsp. red chili flakes

Directions:

1. Blend all of the components for the marinade and marinate veal fingers for 30 minutes.
2. Blend the breadcrumbs, oregano and red chili flakes and add the marinated fingers on this mix.
3. Preheat the Air Fryer to 160 F and cook for 15 minutes, shaking the fry basket occasionally.

Nutrition Info:

- Calories: 121 Protein: 9.9g Fiber: 0.6g Fat: 6.7g Carbs: 3.8g

Chicken Tenders

Servings: 3 | Cooking Time:20 Minutes

Ingredients:

- Chicken tenderloins: 4 cups
- Eggs: one
- Superfine Almond Flour: ½ cup
- Powdered Parmesan cheese: ½ cup
- Kosher Sea salt: ½ teaspoon
- (1-teaspoon) freshly ground black pepper
- (1/2 teaspoon) Cajun seasoning,

Directions:

1. On a small plate, pour the beaten egg.
2. Mix all ingredients in a ziploc bag. Almond flour freshly ground black pepper & kosher salt and other seasonings.
3. Spray the air fryer with oil spray.
4. To avoid clumpy fingers with breading and egg. Use different hands for egg and breading. Dip each tender in egg and then in bread until they are all breaded.
5. Using a fork to place one tender at a time. Bring it in the ziploc bag and shake the bag forcefully. make sure all the tenders are covered in almond mixture
6. Using the fork to take out the tender and place it in your air fryer basket.
7. Spray oil on the tenders.
8. Cook for 12 minutes at 350F, or before 160F registers within. Raise temperature to 400F to shade the surface for 3 minutes.
9. Serve with sauce.

Nutrition Info:

- Calories 280 |Proteins 20g |Carbs 6g|Fat 10g |Fiber 5g

Air Fried Cheesy Chicken Omelet

Servings: 2 | Cooking Time: 18 Minutes

Ingredients:

- Cooked Chicken Breast: half cup (diced) divided
- Four eggs
- Onion powder: 1/4 tsp, divided
- Salt: 1/2 tsp., divided
- Pepper: 1/4 tsp., divided
- Shredded cheese: 2 tbsp. divided
- Garlic powder: 1/4 tsp, divided

Directions:

1. Take two ramekins, grease with olive oil.
2. Add two eggs to each ramekin. Add cheese with seasoning.
3. Blend to combine. Add 1/4 cup of cooked chicken on top.
4. Cook for 14-18 minutes, in the air fryer at 330 F, or until fully cooked.

Nutrition Info:

- Calories 185 |Proteins 20g |Carbs 10g |Fat 5g |

Fried Garlic Green Tomatoes

Servings:2 | Cooking Time: 12 Minutes

Ingredients:

- sliced green tomatoes
- 1/2 cup almond flour
- 2 beaten eggs
- Salt and pepper
- 1 tsp. minced garlic

Directions:

1. Season the tomatoes with salt, garlic, and pepper.
2. Preheat your air fryer to 400°F.
3. Dip the tomatoes first in flour then in the egg mixture.
4. Spray the tomato rounds with olive oil and place in the air fryer basket.
5. Cook for 8 minutes, then flip over and cook for an additional 4 minutes. Serve.

Nutrition Info:

- Calories: 123 kcal; Fat: 3.9g; Carbs: 16g; Protein: 8.4g

Air Fryer Sweet Potato Fries

Servings: 2 | Cooking Time: 8 Minutes

Ingredients:

- One sweet potato
- Pinch of kosher salt and freshly ground black pepper
- 1 tsp olive oil

Directions:

1. Cut the peeled sweet potato in French fries. Coat with salt, pepper, and oil.
2. Cook in the air fryer for 8 minutes, at 400 degrees. Cook potatoes in batches, in single layers.
3. Shake once or twice.
4. Serve with your favorite sauce.

Nutrition Info:

- Calories: 60 | Carbohydrates: 13g | Protein: 1g | fat 6g

Cheese Chicken Fries

Ingredients:

- 1 lb. chicken
- For the marinade:
- 1 tbsp. olive oil
- 1 tsp. mixed herbs
- ½ -tsp. red chili flakes
- A pinch of salt to taste
- 1 tbsp. lemon juice
- For the garnish:
- 1 cup melted cheddar

Directions:

1. Mix all the marinade ingredients well
2. Cook the chicken tenders and in the marinade.
3. Preheat the Air Fryer to 300 F. Take the basket of the

fryer and place the chicken strips in them.
4. Close the container. Cook for 20 or 25 minutes. Toss 2-3 times.
5. Sprinkle the cut coriander leaves on the fries.
6. Pour the melted cheese over the fries and serve hot.

Nutrition Info:

- Calories: 11 Protein: 0.2g Fiber: 0.1g Fat: 0.7g Carbs: 1.0g

Roasted Tomatoes

Servings: 4 | Cooking Time: 15 Minutes

Ingredients:

- 4 tomatoes; halved
- ½ cup parmesan; grated
- 1 tbsp. basil; chopped.
- ½ tsp. onion powder
- ½ tsp. oregano; dried
- ½ tsp. smoked paprika
- ½ tsp. garlic powder
- Cooking spray

Directions:

1. Get a bowl and mix all the ingredients except the cooking spray and the parmesan.
2. Arrange the tomatoes in your air fryer's pan, sprinkle the parmesan on top and grease with cooking spray
3. Cook at 370°F for 15 minutes, divide between plates and serve.

Nutrition Info:

- Calories: 200 Fat: 7g Fiber: 2g Carbs: 4g Protein: 6g

Zucchini Parmesan Chips

Servings: 6 | Cooking Time:20 Minutes

Ingredients:

- Seasoned, whole wheat Breadcrumbs: ½ cup
- Thinly slices of two zucchinis
- Parmesan Cheese: ½ cup (grated)
- 1 Egg whisked
- Kosher salt and pepper, to taste

Directions:

1. Pat dry the zucchini slices so that no moisture remains.
2. In a bowl, whisk the egg with a few tsp. of water and salt, pepper. In another bowl, mix the grated cheese, smoked paprika (optional), and breadcrumbs.
3. Coat zucchini slices in egg mix then in breadcrumbs. Put all in a rack and spray with olive oil.
4. In a single layer, add in the air fryer, and cook for 8 minutes at 350 F. add kosher salt and pepper on top if needed, enjoy as a mid-day snack.

Nutrition Info:

- Cal 101|Fat: 8g|Net Carbs: 6g|Protein: 10g

Crispy Air Fryer Brussels Sprouts

Servings: 4 | Cooking Time: 10 Minutes

Ingredients:

- Almonds sliced: 1/4 cup
- Brussel sprouts: 2 cups
- Kosher salt
- Parmesan cheese: 1/4 cup grated
- Olive oil: 2 Tablespoons
- Everything bagel seasoning: 2 Tablespoons

Directions:

1. In a saucepan, add Brussel sprouts with two cups of water and let it cook over medium flame for almost ten minutes.
2. Drain the sprouts and cut in half.
3. In a mixing bowl, add sliced brussel sprout with crushed almonds, oil, salt, parmesan cheese, and everything bagel seasoning.
4. Completely coat the sprouts.
5. Cook in the air fryer for 12-15 minutes at 375 F or until light brown.
6. Serve hot.

Nutrition Info:

- Calories: 155kcal | Carbohydrates: 3g | Protein: 6g | Fat: 3g |

Radish Chips

Servings: 2 | Cooking Time: 20 Minutes

Ingredients:

- 8 ounces radish slices
- ½ teaspoon garlic powder
- 1 teaspoon salt
- ½ teaspoon onion powder
- ½ teaspoon ground black pepper

Directions:

1. Wash the radish slices, pat them dry, place them in a fryer basket, and then spray oil on them until well coated.
2. Sprinkle salt, garlic powder, onion powder, and black pepper over radish slices and then toss until well coated.
3. Switch on the air fryer, insert fryer basket, then shut with its lid, set the fryer at 370 degrees F and cook for 10 minutes, stirring the slices halfway through.
4. Then spray oil on radish slices, shake the basket and continue frying for 10 minutes, stirring the chips halfway through.
5. Serve straight away.

Nutrition Info:

- Calories: 21 CalCarbs: 1 gFat: 1.8 gProtein: 0.2 gFiber: 0.4 g

Pork Sticks

Servings: 2 | Cooking Time: 15 Minutes

Ingredients:

- 1 lb. boneless pork
- 2 cup dry breadcrumbs
- 2 tsp. oregano
- 2- tsp. red chili flakes
- Marinade:
- 1 ½- tbsp. ginger-garlic paste
- 4- tbsp. lemon juice
- 2- tsp. salt
- 1 tsp. pepper powder
- 1 tsp. red chili powder
- 6- tbsp. corn flour
- 4- eggs

Directions:

1. Blend all marinade ingredients and soak the meat for 20-30 minutes.
2. Blend the breadcrumbs, oregano and red chili well and dip the marinated fingers in this mix.
3. Preheat the Air Fryer to 160 F for 5 minutes.
4. Cook for 15 minutes, shaking halfway through.

Nutrition Info:

- Calories 725 Fat 57 g Carbohydrates 4 g Sugar 0.7 g Protein 49 g Cholesterol 108 mg

Cheese And Veggie Air Fryer Egg Cups

Servings: 4 | Cooking Time: 20 Minutes

Ingredients:

- Shredded cheese: 1 cup
- Non-stick cooking spray
- Vegetables: 1 cup diced
- Chopped cilantro: 1 Tbsp.
- Half and a half: 4 Tbsp.
- Four large eggs
- Salt and Pepper to taste

Directions:

1. Take four ramekins, grease them with oil.
2. In a bowl, crack the eggs with half the cheese, cilantro, salt, diced vegetables, half and half, and pepper.
3. Pour in the ramekins. And put in the air-fryer basket and cook for 12 minutes, at 300 F
4. Then add the cheese to the cups.
5. Let the air-fryer pre-heat for two minutes, at 400 degrees F.
6. Until cheese is lightly browned and melted.
7. Serve hot.

Nutrition Info:

- Calories: 195kcal | Carbohydrates: 7g | Protein: 13g | Fat: 12g |

Vegan Breakfast Sandwich

Servings: 4 | Cooking Time: 10 Minutes

Ingredients:

- Tofu (Egg)
- Garlic powder: 1 teaspoon
- Light soy sauce: 1/4 cup
- Turmeric: 1/2 teaspoon
- 1 block extra firm pressed tofu: cut into 4 round slices
- Breakfast Sandwich
- English muffins: four pieces, vegan
- Avocado: one cut into slices
- Tomato slices
- Vegan cheese: 4 slices
- Sliced onions
- Vegan mayonnaise or vegan butter

Directions:

1. Let the tofu marinate overnight.
2. In a deep dish, add the tofu circles with turmeric, soy sauce, and garlic powder. Let it for 10 minutes or overnight.
3. Put the tofu (marinated) in an air fryer. Cook for ten minutes at 400 F. shake the basket after 5 minutes.
4. Add vegan butter or vegan mayonnaise to the English muffins. Add vegan cheese, avocado slices, tomato, onions slices, and marinated, cooked tofu. Top with the other half of the English muffin.
5. Serve right away and enjoy.

Nutrition Info:

- Cal 198|fat 10 g| carbs 12 g| protein 19.9 g

Parmesan Zucchini Rounds

Servings: 4 | Cooking Time: 20 Minutes

Ingredients:

- 4 zucchinis; sliced
- 1 ½ cups parmesan; grated
- ¼ cup parsley; chopped.
- 1 egg; whisked
- 1 egg white; whisked
- ½ tsp. garlic powder
- Cooking spray

Directions:

1. Get a bowl and mix the egg with egg whites, parmesan, parsley and garlic powder and whisk.
2. Dredge each zucchini slice in this mix, place them all in your air fryer's basket, grease them with cooking spray and cook at 370°F for 20 minutes
3. Divide between plates and serve as a side dish.

Nutrition Info:

- Calories: 183 Fat: 6g Fiber: 2g Carbs: 3g Protein: 8g

Fish Fingers

Servings: 4 | Cooking Time: 15 Minutes

Ingredients:

- ½- lb. firm white fish fillet
- 1 tbsp. lemon juice
- 2 cups of dry breadcrumbs
- 1 cup oil for frying
- Marinade:
- 1 ½- tbsp. ginger-garlic paste
- 3- tbsp. lemon juice
- 2 tsp salt
- 1 ½- tsp pepper powder
- 1 tsp red chili flakes to taste
- 3 eggs
- 5 tbsp. corn flour
- 2 tsp tomato ketchup

Directions:

1. Blend all marinade ingredients and soak the meat for 20-30 minutes.
2. Blend the breadcrumbs, oregano and red chili well and dip the marinated fingers in this mix.
3. Preheat the Air Fryer to 160 F for 5 minutes.
4. Cook for 15 minutes, shaking halfway through.

Nutrition Info:

- Calories 420 Fat 27.4 g Carbohydrates 2 g Sugar 0.3 g Protein 46.3 g Cholesterol 98

Balsamic Cabbage

Servings: 4 | Cooking Time: Minutes

Ingredients:

- 6 cups red cabbage; shredded
- 4 garlic cloves; minced
- 1 tbsp. olive oil
- 1 tbsp. balsamic vinegar
- Salt and black pepper to taste.

Directions:

1. In a pan that fits the air fryer, combine all the ingredients, toss, introduce the pan in the air fryer and cook at 380°F for 15 minutes
2. Divide between plates and serve as a side dish.

Nutrition Info:

- Calories: 151 Fat: 2g Fiber: 3g Carbs: 5g Protein: 5g

Air Fryer Spanakopita Bites

Servings: 4 | Cooking Time:15 Minutes

Ingredients:

- 4 sheets phyllo dough
- Baby spinach leaves: 2 cups
- Grated Parmesan cheese: 2 tablespoons
- Low-fat cottage cheese: 1/4 cup
- Dried oregano: 1 teaspoon
- Feta cheese: 6 tbsp. crumbled
- Water: 2 tablespoons
- One egg white only
- Lemon zest: 1 teaspoon
- Cayenne pepper: 1/8 teaspoon
- Olive oil: 1 tablespoon
- Kosher salt and freshly ground black pepper: 1/4 teaspoon, each

Directions:

1. In a pot over high heat, add water and spinach, cook until wilted.
2. Drain it and cool for ten minutes. Squeeze out excess moisture.
3. In a bowl, mix cottage cheese, Parmesan cheese, oregano, salt, cayenne pepper, egg white, freshly ground black pepper, feta cheese, spinach, and zest. Mix it well or in the food processor.
4. Lay one phyllo sheet on a flat surface. Spray with oil. Add the second sheet of phyllo on top—spray oil. Add a total of 4 oiled sheets.
5. Form 16 strips from these four oiled sheets. Add one tbsp of filling in one strip. Roll it around the filling.
6. Spray the air fryer basket with oil. Put eight bites in the basket, spray with oil. Cook for 12 minutes at 375°F until crispy and golden brown. Flip halfway through.
7. Serve hot.

Nutrition Info:

- Calories 82|Fat 4g|Protein 4g|Carbohydrate 7g

Air Fryer Bacon-wrapped Jalapeno Poppers

Servings: 10 | Cooking Time: 8 Minutes

Ingredients:

- Cream cheese: 1/3 cup
- Ten jalapenos
- Thin bacon: 5 strips

Directions:

1. Wash and pat dry the jalapenos. Cut them in half and take out the seeds.
2. Add the cream cheese in the middle, but do not put too much
3. Let the air fryer preheat to 370 F. cut the bacon strips in half.
4. Wrap the cream cheese filled jalapenos with slices of bacon.
5. Secure with a toothpick.
6. Place the wrapped jalapenos in an air fryer, cook at 370 F and cook for 6-8 minutes or until the bacon is crispy.
7. Serve hot.

Nutrition Info:

- Calories: 76kcal | Carbohydrates: 1g | Protein: 2g | Fat: 7g |

Air Fryer Avocado Fries

Servings: 2 | Cooking Time: 10 Minutes

Ingredients:

- One avocado
- One egg
- Whole wheat bread crumbs: 1/2 cup
- Salt: 1/2 teaspoon

Directions:

1. Avocado should be firm and firm. Cut into wedges.
2. In a bowl, beat egg with salt. In another bowl, add the crumbs.
3. Coat wedges in egg, then in crumbs.
4. Air fry them at 400F for 8-10 minutes. Toss halfway through.
5. Serve hot.

Nutrition Info:

- Calories: 251kcal | Carbohydrates: 19g | Protein: 6g | Fat: 17g |

Air Fryer Egg Rolls

Servings: 3 | Cooking Time:20 Minutes

Ingredients:

- Coleslaw mix: half bag
- Half onion
- Salt: 1/2 teaspoon
- Half cups of mushrooms
- Lean ground pork: 2 cups
- One stalk of celery
- Wrappers (egg roll)

Directions:

1. Put a skillet over medium flame, add onion and lean ground pork and cook for 5-7 minutes
2. Add coleslaw mixture, salt, mushrooms, and celery to skillet and cook for almost five minutes
3. Lay egg roll wrapper flat and add filling (1/3 cup), roll it up, seal with water.
4. Spray with oil the rolls.
5. Put in the air fryer for 6-8 minutes at 400F, flipping once halfway through.
6. Serve hot.

Nutrition Info:

- Cal 245| Fat: 10g| Net Carbs: 9g|Protein: 11g

Jicama Fries

Servings: 4 | Cooking Time: 20 Minutes

Ingredients:

- 1 small jicama; peeled.
- ¼ tsp. onion powder.
- ¾tsp. chili powder
- ¼ tsp. ground black pepper
- ¼ tsp. garlic powder.

Directions:

1. Cut jicama into matchstick-sized pieces.
2. Place pieces into a small bowl and sprinkle with remaining ingredients. Place the fries into the air fryer basket
3. Modify the temperature to 350 Degrees F and set the timer for 20 minutes. Toss the basket two or three times during cooking. Serve warm.

Nutrition Info:

- Calories: 37 Protein: 0.8g Fiber: 4.7g Fat: 0.1g Carbs: 8.7g

Chapter 4: Poultry Recipes

Chapter 4: Poultry Recipes

Chicken Wings With Garlic Parmesan

Servings: 3 | Cooking Time: 25 Minutes

Ingredients:

- 25g cornstarch
- 20g grated Parmesan cheese
- 9g garlic powder
- Salt and pepper to taste
- 680g chicken wings
- Nonstick Spray Oil

Directions:

1. Select Preheat, set the temperature to 200 °C and press Start / Pause.
2. Combine corn starch, Parmesan, garlic powder, salt, and pepper in a bowl.
3. Mix the chicken wings in the seasoning and dip until well coated.
4. Spray the baskets and the air fryer with oil spray and add the wings, sprinkling the tops of the wings as well.
5. Select Chicken and press Start/Pause. Be sure to shake the baskets in the middle of cooking.
6. Sprinkle with what's left of the Parmesan mix and serve.

Nutrition Info:

- Calories: 204 Fat: 15g Carbohydrates: 1g Proteins: 12g Sugar: 0g Cholesterol: 63mg

No-breading Chicken Breast In Air Fryer

Servings: 2 | Cooking Time:20 Minutes

Ingredients:

- Olive oil spray
- Chicken breasts: 4 (boneless)
- Onion powder: 3/4 teaspoon
- Salt: ¼ cup
- Smoked paprika: half tsp.
- 1/8 tsp. of cayenne pepper
- Garlic powder: 3/4 teaspoon
- Dried parsley: half tsp.

Directions:

1. In a large bowl, add six cups of warm water, add salt (1/4 cup) and mix to dissolve.
2. Put chicken breasts in the warm salted water and let it refrigerate for almost 2 hours.
3. Remove from water and pat dry.
4. In a bowl, add all the spices with ¾ tsp. of salt. Spray the oil all over the chicken and rub the spice mix all over the chicken.
5. Let the air fryer heat at 380F.
6. Put the chicken in the air fryer and cook for ten minutes.

Flip halfway through and serve with salad green.

Nutrition Info:

- Calories: 208kcal|Carbohydrates: 1g| Protein: 39g| Fat: 4.5g

Air Fried Blackened Chicken Breast

Servings: 2 | Cooking Time:20 Minutes

Ingredients:

- Paprika: 2 teaspoons
- Ground thyme: 1 teaspoon
- Cumin: 1 teaspoon
- Cayenne pepper: half tsp.
- Onion powder: half tsp.
- Black Pepper: half tsp.
- Salt: ¼ teaspoon
- Vegetable oil: 2 teaspoons
- Pieces of chicken breast halves (without bones and skin)

Directions:

1. In a mixing bowl, add onion powder, salt, cumin, paprika, black pepper, thyme, and cayenne pepper. Mix it well.
2. Drizzle oil over chicken and rub. Dip each piece of chicken in blackening spice blend on both sides.
3. Let it rest for five minutes while the air fryer is preheating.
4. Preheat it for five minutes at 360F.
5. Put the chicken in the air fryer and let it cook for ten minutes. Flip and then cook for another ten minutes.
6. After, let it sit for five minutes, then slice and serve with the side of greens.

Nutrition Info:

- 432.1 calories| protein 79.4g| carbohydrates 3.2g| fat 9.5g

Air Fried Chicken Fajitas

Servings: 6 | Cooking Time:20 Minutes

Ingredients:

- Chicken breasts: 4 cups, cut into thin strips
- Bell peppers, sliced
- Salt: half tsp.
- Cumin: 1 tsp.
- Garlic powder: 1/4 tsp
- Chili powder: half tsp.
- Lime juice: 1 tbsp.

Directions:

1. In a bowl, add seasonings, chicken and lime juice, and mix well.
2. Then add sliced peppers and coat well.
3. Spray the air fryer with olive oil.
4. Put the chicken and peppers in, and cook for 15 minutes

at 400 F. flip halfway through.

5. Serve with wedges of lemons and enjoy.

Nutrition Info:

• Calories 140 |Proteins 22g |Carbs 6g|Fat 5g |Fiber 7g

Chicken Soup

Servings: 6 | Cooking Time: 1 Hour 20 Minutes

Ingredients:

• 4 lbs Chicken, cut into pieces
• 5 carrots, sliced thick
• 8 cups of water
• 2 celery stalks, sliced 1 inch thick
• 2 large onions, sliced

Directions:

1. In a large pot add chicken, water, and salt. Bring to boil.
2. Add celery and onion in the pot and stir well.
3. Turn heat to medium-low and simmer for 30 minutes.
4. Add carrots and cover pot with a lid and simmer for 40 minutes.
5. Remove Chicken from the pot and remove bones and cut Chicken into bite-size pieces.
6. Return chicken into the pot and stir well.
7. Serve and enjoy.

Nutrition Info:

• Calories: 89 Fat: 6.33gCarbohydrates: 0g Protein: 7.56g Sugar: 0g Cholesterol: 0mg

Garlic Parmesan Chicken Tenders

Servings: 4 | Cooking Time:12 Minutes

Ingredients:

• One egg
• Eight raw chicken tenders
• Water: 2 tablespoons
• Olive oil
• To coat
• Panko breadcrumbs: 1 cup
• Half tsp of salt
• Black Pepper: 1/4 teaspoon
• Garlic powder: 1 teaspoon
• Onion powder: 1/2 teaspoon
• Parmesan cheese: 1/4 cup
• Any dipping Sauce

Directions:

1. Add all the coating ingredients in a big bowl
2. In another bowl, mix water and egg.
3. Dip the chicken in the egg mix, then in the coating mix.
4. Put the tenders in the air fry basket in a single layer.
5. Spray with the olive oil light
6. Cook at 400 degrees for 12 minutes. Flip the chicken halfway through.
7. Serve with salad greens and enjoy.

Nutrition Info:

• Calories: 220 | Carbohydrates: 13g | Protein: 27g | Fat: 6g |

Herb Chicken Thighs

Servings: 6 | Cooking Time: 40 Minutes

Ingredients:

• 6 chicken thighs, skin-on, pastured
• 2 teaspoons garlic powder
• 1/2 teaspoon onion powder
• 1 teaspoon dried basil
• 1 teaspoon spike seasoning
• 1/2 teaspoon dried sage
• 1/4 teaspoon ground black pepper
• 1/2 teaspoon dried oregano
• 2 tablespoons lemon juice
• 1/4 cup olive oil

Directions:

1. Prepare the marinade and for this, place all the ingredients in a bowl, except for chicken, stir until well combined and then pour the marinade in a large plastic bag.
2. Add chicken thighs in the plastic bag, seal the bag, then turn in upside down until chicken thighs are coated with the marinade and let marinate in the refrigerator for minimum of 6 hours.
3. Then drain the chicken, arrange the chicken thighs on a wire rack and let them rest for 15 minutes at room temperature.
4. Meanwhile, switch on the air fryer, insert fryer basket, grease it with olive oil, then shut with its lid, set the fryer at 360 degrees F and preheat for 5 minutes.
5. Then open the fryer, add chicken thighs in it in a single layer top-side down, close with its lid, cook the chicken for 8 minutes, turn the chicken, and continue frying for 6 minutes.
6. Turn the chicken thighs and then continue cooking for another 6 minutes or until chicken is nicely browned and cooked.
7. When air fryer beeps, open its lid, transfer chicken onto a serving plate and cook the remaining chicken thighs in the same manner.
8. Serve straight away.

Nutrition Info:

• Calories: 163 CalCarbs: 1 gFat: 9.2 gProtein: 19.4 gFiber: 0.3 g

Chicken Sandwich

Servings: 6 | Cooking Time: 20 Minutes

Ingredients:

• 4 chicken breasts, pastured
• 1 cup almond flour
• ¾ teaspoon ground black pepper
• 1/2 teaspoon paprika
• 1 teaspoon salt

- 1/2 teaspoon celery seeds
- 1 teaspoon potato starch
- 1/4 cup milk, reduced-fat
- 4 cups dill pickle juice as needed
- 2 eggs, pastured
- 4 hamburger buns
- 1/8 teaspoon dry milk powder, nonfat
- ¼ teaspoon xanthan gum
- 1/8 teaspoon erythritol sweetener

Directions:

1. Place the chicken in a large plastic bag, seal the bag and then pound the chicken with a mallet until ½-inch thick.
2. Brine the chicken and for this, pour the dill pickle juice in the plastic bag containing chicken, then seal it and let the chicken soak for a minimum of 2 hours.
3. After 2 hours, remove the chicken from the brine, rinse it well, and pat dry with paper towels.
4. Place flour in a shallow dish, add black pepper, paprika, salt, celery, potato starch, milk powder, xanthan gum, and sweetener and stir until well mixed.
5. Crack eggs in another dish and then whisk until blended.
6. Switch on the air fryer, insert fryer basket, grease it with olive oil, then shut with its lid, set the fryer at 375 degrees F and preheat for 5 minutes.
7. Meanwhile, dip the chicken into the egg and then coat evenly with the flour mixture.
8. Open the fryer, add chicken breasts in it in a single layer, close with its lid, then cook for 10 minutes, flip the chickens and continue cooking for 5 minutes or until chicken is nicely golden and cooked.
9. When air fryer beeps, open its lid, transfer chicken into a plate and cook remaining chicken in the same manner.
10. Sandwich a chicken breast between toasted hamburger buns, top with favorite dressing and serve.

Nutrition Info:

- Calories: 440 CalCarbs: 40 gFat: 19 gProtein: 28 gFiber: 12 g

Cheesy Pork Chops In Air Fryer

Servings: 2 | Cooking Time:8 Minutes

Ingredients:

- 4 lean pork chops
- Salt: half tsp.
- Garlic powder: half tsp.
- Shredded cheese: 4 tbsp.
- Chopped cilantro

Directions:

1. Let the air fryer preheat to 350 degrees.
2. With garlic, cilantro, and salt, rub the pork chops. Put in the air fryer. Let it cook for four minutes. Flip them and cook for two minutes more.
3. Add cheese on top of them and cook for another two minutes or until the cheese is melted.
4. Serve with salad greens.

Nutrition Info:

- Calories: 467kcal | Protein: 61g | Fat: 22g | Saturated Fat: 8g |

Fried Chicken Tamari And Mustard

Servings: 4 | Cooking Time: 1h 20 Minutes

Ingredients:

- 1kg of very small chopped chicken
- Tamari Sauce
- Original mustard
- Ground pepper
- 1 lemon
- Flour
- Extra virgin olive oil

Directions:

1. Put the chicken in a bowl, you can put the chicken with or without the skin, to everyone's taste.
2. Add a generous stream of tamari, one or two tablespoons of mustard, a little ground pepper and a splash of lemon juice.
3. Link everything very well and let macerate an hour.
4. Pass the chicken pieces for flour and place in the air fryer basket.
5. Put 20 minutes at 200 degrees. At half time, move the chicken from the basket.
6. Do not crush the chicken, it is preferable to make two or three batches of chicken to pile up and do not fry the pieces well.

Nutrition Info:

- Calories: 100Fat: 6g Carbohydrates 0gProtein: 18g Sugar: 0g

Chicken's Liver

Servings: 4 | Cooking Time: 30 Minutes

Ingredients:

- 500g of chicken livers
- 2 or 3 carrots
- 1 green pepper
- 1 red pepper
- 1 onion
- 4 tomatoes
- Salt
- Ground pepper
- 1 glass of white wine
- ½ glass of water
- Extra virgin olive oil

Directions:

1. Peel the carrots, cut them into slices and add them to the bowl of the air fryer with a tablespoon of extra virgin olive oil 5 minutes.
2. After 5 minutes, add the peppers and onion in julienne. Select 5 minutes.

3. After that time, add the tomatoes in wedges and select 5 more minutes.
4. Add now the chicken liver clean and chopped.
5. Season, add the wine and water.
6. Select 10 minutes.
7. Check that the liver is tender.

Nutrition Info:

• Calories: 76 Fat: 13g Carbohydrates: 1g Protein: 2Sugar: 1gCholesterol: 130mg

Chicken With Mixed Vegetables

Servings: 2 | Cooking Time:20 Minutes

Ingredients:

• 1/2 onion diced
• Chicken breast: 4 cups, cubed pieces
• Half zucchini chopped
• Italian seasoning: 1 tablespoon
• Bell pepper chopped: 1/2 cup
• Clove of garlic pressed
• Broccoli florets: 1/2 cup
• Olive oil: 2 tablespoons
• Half teaspoon of chili powder, garlic powder, pepper, salt,

Directions:

1. Let the air fryer heat to 400 F and dice the vegetables
2. In a bowl, add the seasoning, oil and add vegetables, chicken and toss well
3. Place chicken and vegetables in the air fryer, and cook for ten minutes, toss half way through, cook in batches.
4. Make sure the veggies are charred and the chicken is cooked through.
5. Serve hot.

Nutrition Info:

• | Calories: 230kcal | Carbohydrates: 8g | Protein: 26g | Fat: 10g |

Chicken Thighs

Servings: 2 | Cooking Time: 20 Minutes

Ingredients:

• 4 chicken thighs
• Salt
• Pepper
• Mustard
• Paprika

Directions:

1. Before using the pot, it is convenient to turn on for 5 minutes to heat it. Marinate the thighs with salt, pepper, mustard, and paprika. Put your thighs in the air fryer for 10 minutes at 3800F
2. After the time, turn the thighs and fry for 10 more minutes. If necessary, you can use an additional 5 minutes depending on the size of the thighs so that they are well cooked.

Nutrition Info:

• Calories: 72 kcal; Fat: 2.36g; Carbs: 0g; Protein: 11.78g

Caribbean Spiced Chicken

Servings: 4 | Cooking Time: 20 Minutes

Ingredients:

• 1.5-pound boneless chicken thigh fillets, skinless, pastured
• ½ tablespoon ground ginger
• ¾ teaspoon ground black pepper
• ½ tablespoon ground nutmeg
• 1 teaspoon salt
• ½ tablespoon cayenne pepper
• ½ tablespoon ground coriander
• ½ tablespoon ground cinnamon
• 1½ tablespoon olive oil

Directions:

1. Meanwhile, take a baking sheet, line it with paper towels, then place chicken on it, season the chicken with salt and black pepper on both sides and let it sit for 30 minutes.
2. Prepare the spice mix and for this, place remaining ingredients in a bowl, except for oil, and then stir well until mixed.
3. Pat dry the chicken, then season well with the spice mix and brush with oil.
4. Switch on the air fryer, insert fryer basket, grease it with olive oil, then shut with its lid, set the fryer at 390 degrees F and preheat for 5 minutes.
5. Then open the fryer, add seasoned chicken in it in a single layer, close with its lid and cook for 10 minutes until nicely golden and cooked, turning the chicken halfway through the frying.
6. When air fryer beeps, open its lid, transfer chicken into a heatproof dish and then cover it with foil to keep the chicken warm.
7. Cook remaining chicken in the same manner and serve.

Nutrition Info:

• Calories: 202 CalCarbs: 1.7 gFat: 13.4 gProtein: 25 gFiber: 0.4 g

Air Fryer Tasty Egg Rolls

Servings: 3 | Cooking Time:20 Minutes

Ingredients:

• Coleslaw mix: half bag
• Half onion
• Salt: 1/2 teaspoon
• Half cups of mushrooms
• Lean ground pork: 2 cups
• One stalk of celery
• Wrappers (egg roll)

Directions:

1. Put a skillet over medium flame, add onion and lean

ground pork and cook for 5-7 minutes.

2. Add coleslaw mixture, salt, mushrooms, and celery to skillet and cook for almost five minutes.

3. Lay egg roll wrapper flat and add filling (1/3 cup), roll it up, seal with water.

4. Spray with oil the rolls.

5. Put in the air fryer for 6-8 minutes at 400F, flipping once halfway through.

6. Serve hot.

Nutrition Info:

- Cal 245| Fat: 10g| Net Carbs: 9g|Protein: 11g

Fried Lemon Chicken

Servings: Six | Cooking Time: 20 Minutes

Ingredients:

- 6 chicken thighs
- 2 tbsp. olive oil
- 2 tbsp. lemon juice
- 1 tbsp. Italian herbal seasoning mix
- 1 tsp. Celtic sea salt
- 1 tsp. ground fresh pepper
- 1 lemon, thinly slice

Directions:

1. Add all ingredients, except sliced lemon, to bowl or bag, stir to cover chicken.

2. Let marinate for 30 minutes overnight.

3. Remove the chicken and let the excess oil drip (it does not need to dry out, just do not drip with tons of excess oil).

4. Arrange the chicken thighs and the lemon slices in the fryer basket, being careful not to push the chicken thighs too close to each other.

5. Set the fryer to 200 degrees and cook for 10 minutes.

6. Remove the basket from the fryer and turn the chicken thighs to the other side.

7. Cook again at 200 for another 10 minutes.

Nutrition Info:

- Calories: 215 Fat: 13g Carbohydrates: 1g Protein: 2Sugar: 1gCholesterol: 130mg

Pesto Chicken

Servings: 6

Ingredients:

- 1 ¾ lbs chicken breasts, skinless, boneless, and slice
- ½ cup mozzarella cheese, shredded
- ¼ cup pesto

Directions:

1. Add chicken and pesto in a mixing bowl and mix until well coated.

2. Place in refrigerator for 2-3 hours.

3. Grill chicken over medium heat until completely cooked.

4. Sprinkle cheese over chicken and serve.

Nutrition Info:

- Calories: 303 Fat: 13g Carbohydrates: 1g Protein: 2Sugar: 1gCholesterol: 122mg

Orange Chicken Wings

Servings: 2 | Cooking Time: 14 Minutes

Ingredients:

- Honey: 1 tbsp.
- Chicken Wings, Six pieces
- One orange zest and juice
- Worcestershire Sauce: 1.5 tbsp.
- Black pepper to taste
- Herbs (sage, rosemary, oregano, parsley, basil, thyme, and mint)

Directions:

1. Wash and pat dry the chicken wings

2. In a bowl, add chicken wings, pour zest and orange juice

3. Add the rest of the ingredients and rub on chicken wings. Let it marinate for at least half an hour.

4. Let the Air fryer preheat at 180°C

5. In an aluminum foil, wrap the marinated wings and put them in an air fryer, and cook for 20 minutes at 180 C

6. After 20 minutes, remove aluminum foil and brush the sauce over wings and cook for 15 minutes more. Then again, brush the sauce and cook for another ten minutes.

7. Take out from the air fryer and serve hot.

Nutrition Info:

- Calories 271 |Proteins 29g |Carbs 20g |Fat 15g |

Ham And Cheese Stuffed Chicken Burgers

Servings:4

Ingredients:

- ⅓ Cup soft bread crumbs
- 3 tablespoons milk
- 1 egg, beaten
- ½ teaspoon dried thyme
- Pinch salt
- Freshly ground black pepper
- 1¼ pounds ground chicken
- ¼ cup finely chopped ham
- ⅓ cup grated Havarti cheese
- Olive oil for misting

Directions:

1. In a medium bowl, combine the breadcrumbs, milk, egg, thyme, salt, and pepper. Add the chicken and mix gently but thoroughly with clean hands.

2. Form the chicken into eight thin patties and place on waxed paper.

3. Top four of the patties with the ham and cheese. Top with remaining four patties and gently press the edges together to seal, so the ham and cheese mixture is in the middle of the burger.

4. Place the burgers in the basket and mist with olive oil. Grill for 13 to 16 minutes or until the chicken is thoroughly cooked to 165°F as measured with a meat thermometer.

Nutrition Info:
- Calories: 324 Fat: 13g Carbohydrates: 1g Protein: 2Sugar: 1gCholesterol: 130mg

Lemon-garlic Chicken

Servings: 4 | Cooking Time: 35 Minutes

Ingredients:
- Lemon juice ¼ cup
- 1 Tbsp. olive oil
- 1 tsp mustard
- Cloves of garlic
- ¼ tsp salt
- ⅛ tsp black pepper
- Chicken thighs
- Lemon wedges

Directions:

1. In a bowl, whisk together the olive oil, lemon juice, mustard Dijon, garlic, salt, and pepper.
2. Place the chicken thighs in a large ziploc bag. Spill marinade over chicken & seal bag, ensuring all chicken parts are covered. Cool for at least 2 hours.
3. Preheat a frying pan to 360 F (175 C).
4. Remove the chicken with towels from the marinade, & pat dry.
5. Place pieces of chicken in the air fryer basket, if necessary, cook them in batches.
6. Fry till chicken is no longer pink on the bone & the juices run smoothly, 22 to 24 min. Upon serving, press a lemon slice across each piece.

Nutrition Info:
- Cal 258|Fat: 18.6g| Carbs: 3.6g| Protein: 19.4g

Southwest Chicken In Air Fryer

Servings: 4 | Cooking Time:30 Minutes

Ingredients:
- Avocado oil: one tbsp.
- Four cups of boneless, skinless, chicken breast
- Chili powder: half tsp.
- Salt to taste
- Cumin: half tsp.
- Onion powder: 1/4 tsp.
- Lime juice: two tbsp.
- Garlic powder: 1/4 tsp

Directions:

1. In a ziploc bag, add chicken, oil, and lime juice.
2. Add all spices in a bowl and rub all over the chicken in the ziploc bag.
3. Let it marinate in the fridge for ten minutes or more.
4. Take chicken out from the ziploc bag and put it in the air

fryer.
5. Cook for 25 minutes at 400 F, flipping chicken halfway through until internal temperature reaches 165 degrees.

Nutrition Info:
- Calories: 165kcal|Carbohydrates: 1g|Protein: 24g|Fat: 6g

Buffalo Chicken Hot Wings

Servings: 6 | Cooking Time: 45 Minutes

Ingredients:
- 16 chicken wings, pastured
- 1 teaspoon garlic powder
- 2 teaspoons chicken seasoning
- ¾ teaspoon ground black pepper
- 2 teaspoons soy sauce
- 1/4 cup buffalo sauce, reduced-fat

Directions:

1. Switch on the air fryer, insert fryer basket, grease it with olive oil, then shut with its lid, set the fryer at 400 degrees F and preheat for 5 minutes.
2. Meanwhile, place chicken wings in a bowl, drizzle with soy sauce, toss until well coated and then season with black pepper and garlic powder.
3. Open the fryer, stack chicken wings in it, then spray with oil and close with its lid.
4. Cook the chicken wings for 10 minutes, turning the wings halfway through, and then transfer them to a bowl, covering the bowl with a foil to keep the chicken wings warm.
5. Air fry the remaining chicken wings in the same manner, then transfer them to the bowl, add buffalo sauce and toss until well coated.
6. Return chicken wings into the fryer basket in a single layer and continue frying for 7 to 12 minutes or until chicken wings are glazed and crispy, shaking the chicken wings every 3 to 4 minutes.
7. Serve straight away.

Nutrition Info:
- Calories: 88 CalCarbs: 2.6 gFat: 6.5 gProtein: 4.5 gFiber: 0.1 g

Air Fryer Bbq Cheddar- Stuffed Hen Breasts

Servings: 2 | Cooking Time: 25 Minutes

Ingredients:
- 3 strips separated bacon
- 2 oz. cubed and divided Cheddar cheese
- 1/4 cup separated barbeque sauce
- 4 oz. Skinless, boneless hen breasts.
- Salt and ground black pepper

Directions:

1. Cook 1 strip of bacon in the air fryer for 2 minutes. Line

the air fryer basket with parchment paper and increase the temperature to 400F.
2. Combine prepared bacon, Cheddar cheese, and also 1 tbsp. barbeque sauce in a bowl.
3. Cover continuing to be strips of bacon around each chicken bust. Coat the breast with remaining barbeque sauce and set into the ready air fryer basket
4. Cook for 10 mins in the air fryer, turn, and also proceed cooking till chicken is no more pink in the facility as well as the juices run clear, about 10 even more minutes.
5. An instant-read thermostat placed into the facility needs to check out at least 165 F.

Nutrition Info:
- Calories: 379 kcal; Carbs:12.3g; Protein:37.7g; Fat: 18.9g

Crispy Chicken Wings

Servings: 4 | Cooking Time: 20 Minutes

Ingredients:
- 1 tbsp. Gluten-free baking powder
- 3/4 tsp. Sea salt
- 2 lbs. Chicken wings
- 1/4 tsp. Black pepper

Directions:
1. Preheat the Air Fryer to 3700F. Merge the chicken wings, baking powder, sea salt, and black pepper.
2. Pour some grease on the Air Fryer basket. Arrange the wings in batches into the Air Fryer basket and cook for at 2500F for 15 minutes.
3. Shake the Air Fryer or turn the wings to the other side and cook for another 15 minutes for the wings to be well cooked.
4. Serve.

Nutrition Info:
- Calories: 275 kcal; Carbs: 9g; Fat: 17g; Proteins: 13g

Chicken Nuggets

Servings: 4 | Cooking Time: 24 Minutes

Ingredients:
- 1-pound chicken breast, pastured
- 1/4 cup coconut flour
- 6 tablespoons toasted sesame seeds
- 1/2 teaspoon ginger powder
- 1/8 teaspoon sea salt
- 1 teaspoon sesame oil
- 4 egg whites, pastured

Directions:
1. Switch on the air fryer, insert fryer basket, grease it with olive oil, then shut with its lid, set the fryer at 400 degrees F and preheat for 10 minutes.
2. Meanwhile, cut the chicken breast into 1-inch pieces, pat them dry, place the chicken pieces in a bowl, sprinkle with salt and oil and toss until well coated.

3. Place flour in a large plastic bag, add ginger and chicken, seal the bag and turn it upside down to coat the chicken with flour evenly.
4. Place egg whites in a bowl, whisk well, then add coated chicken and toss until well coated.
5. Place sesame seeds in a large plastic bag, add chicken pieces in it, seal the bag and turn it upside down to coat the chicken with sesame seeds evenly.
6. Open the fryer, add chicken nuggets in it in a single layer, spray with oil, close with its lid and cook for 12 minutes until nicely golden and cooked, turning the chicken nuggets and spraying with oil halfway through.
7. When air fryer beeps, open its lid, transfer chicken nuggets onto a serving plate and fry the remaining chicken nuggets in the same manner.
8. Serve straight away.

Nutrition Info:
- Calories: 312 CalCarbs: 9 gFat: 15 gProtein: 33.6 gFiber: 5 g

Crispy Chicken Thighs

Servings: 2 | Cooking Time: 20 Minutes

Ingredients:
- chicken thighs, skin on, bone removed, pat dry
- salt
- garlic powder
- black pepper

Directions:
1. Preheat the Air Fryer to 4000F. Season the chicken with salt and pepper. Place the chicken in the Air Fryer basket.
2. Cook at 4000F for 18 minutes and top with black pepper.
3. Serve.

Nutrition Info:
- Calories: 104 kcal; Protein: 13.5g; Carbs: 0g; Fat: 5.7g

Breaded Chicken With Seed Chips

Servings: 4 | Cooking Time: 40 Minutes

Ingredients:
- 12 chicken breast fillets
- Salt
- 2 eggs
- 1 small bag of seed chips
- Breadcrumbs
- Extra virgin olive oil

Directions:
1. Put salt to chicken fillets.
2. Crush the seed chips and when we have them fine, bind with the breadcrumbs.
3. Beat the two eggs.
4. Pass the chicken breast fillets through the beaten egg and then through the seed chips that you have tied with the breadcrumbs.

5. When you have them all breaded, paint with a brush of extra virgin olive oil.
6. Place the fillets in the basket of the air fryer without being piled up.
7. Select 170 degrees, 20 minutes.
8. Take out and put another batch, repeat temperature and time. So, until you use up all the steaks.

Nutrition Info:
• Calories: 242 Fat: 13g Carbohydrates: 13.5g Protein: 18g Sugar: 0g Cholesterol: 42mg

Air Fryer Barbeque Cheddar-stuffed Poultry Breasts

Servings: 2 | Cooking Time: 25 Minutes

Ingredients:
• 3 divided strips bacon
• 2 oz. cubed cheddar cheese
• 1/4 mug split BBQ sauce
• 4 oz. skinless, boneless poultry breasts.
• Salt and black pepper

Directions:
1. Adjust the temperature of the air fryer to 380ºF. Prepare 1 strip of bacon in the air fryer for 2 mins. Eliminate from air fryer and also cut into small items. Line the air fryer and boost the temperature to 400F.
2. Integrate cooked bacon, Cheddar cheese, and also 1 tbsp. BBQ sauce in a bowl.
3. Utilize a long, sharp knife to make a horizontal 1-inch cut on top of each breast, producing a little interior bag. Stuff each bust just as with the bacon-cheese combination. Wrap continuing to be strips of bacon around each chicken bust. Coat the breast with remaining barbecue sauce and set it right into the ready air fryer basket.
4. Cook for 10 minutes in the air fryer, turn as well as proceed food preparation till chicken is no pinker in the center, and the juices run clear concerning 10 more minutes. An instant-read thermostat placed into the center needs to check out at the very least 165F.

Nutrition Info:
• Calories: 379 kcal; Carbs: 12.3g; Protein: 37.7g; Fat:18.9g

Salted Biscuit Pie Turkey Chops

Servings: 4 | Cooking Time: 20 Minutes

Ingredients:
• 8 large turkey chops
• 300 gr of crackers
• 2 eggs
• Extra virgin olive oil
• Salt
• Ground pepper

Directions:

1. Put the turkey chops on the worktable, and salt and pepper.
2. Beat the eggs in a bowl.
3. Crush the cookies in the Thermo mix with a few turbo strokes until they are made grit, or you can crush them with the blender.
4. Put the cookies in a bowl.
5. Pass the chops through the beaten egg and then passed them through the crushed cookies. Press well so that the empanada is perfect.
6. Paint the empanada with a silicone brush and extra virgin olive oil.
7. Put the chops in the basket of the air fryer, not all will enter. They will be done in batches.
8. Select 200 degrees, 15 minutes.
9. When you have all the chops made, serve.

Nutrition Info:
• Calories: 126 Fat: 6g Carbohydrates 0gProtein: 18g Sugar: 0g

Chicken Cheesey Quesadilla In Air Fryer

Servings: 4 | Cooking Time: 7 Minutes

Ingredients:
• Precooked chicken: one cup, diced
• Tortillas: 2 pieces
• Low-fat cheese: one cup (shredded)

Directions:
1. Spray oil the air basket and place one tortilla in it. Add cooked chicken and cheese on top.
2. Add the second tortilla on top. Put a metal rack on top.
3. Cook for 6 minutes at 370 degrees, flip it halfway through so cooking evenly.
4. Slice and serve with dipping sauce.

Nutrition Info:
• Calories: 171kcal | Carbohydrates: 8g | Protein: 15g | Fat: 8g |

Jamaican Jerk Pork In Air Fryer

Servings: 4 | Cooking Time:20 Minutes

Ingredients:
• Pork, cut into three-inch pieces
• Jerk paste: ¼ cup

Directions:
1. Rub jerk paste all over the pork pieces.
2. Let it marinate for four hours, at least, in the refrigerator. Or for more time.
3. Let the air fryer preheat to 390 F. spray with olive oil
4. Before putting in the air fryer, let the meat sit for 20 minutes at room temperature.
5. Cook for 20 minutes at 390 F in the air fryer, flip half-

way through.
6. Take out from the air fryer let it rest for ten minutes before slicing.
7. Serve with microgreens.

Nutrition Info:

- Calories: 234kcal | Protein: 31g | Fat: 9g |carbs 12 g

Lemon Chicken With Basil

Servings: 4 | Cooking Time: 1h

Ingredients:

- 1kg chopped chicken
- 2 lemons
- Basil, salt and ground pepper
- Extra virgin olive oil

Directions:

1. Put the chicken in a bowl with a jet of extra virgin olive oil.
2. Put salt, pepper, and basil.
3. Bind well and let stand for at least 30 minutes, stirring occasionally.
4. Put the pieces of chicken in the air fryer basket and take the air fryer
5. Select 30 minutes.
6. Occasionally remove.
7. Take out and put another batch.
8. Repeat the same process.

Nutrition Info:

- Calories: 1,440 kcal; Fat: 74.9g; Carbs: 122.0g; Protein: 68.6g

Garlic-roasted Chicken With Creamer Potatoes

Servings:4

Ingredients:

- 1 (2½-to 3-pound) broiler-fryer whole chicken
- 2 tablespoons olive oil
- ½-teaspoon garlic salt
- 8 cloves garlic, peeled
- 1 slice lemon
- ½ teaspoon dried thyme
- ½ teaspoon dried marjoram
- 12 to 16 creamer potatoes, scrubbed

Directions:

1. Do not wash the chicken before cooking. Remove it from its packaging and pat the chicken dry.
2. Combine the olive oil and salt in a small bowl. Rub half of this mixture on the inside of the chicken, under the skin, and on the chicken skin. Place the garlic cloves and lemon slice inside the chicken. Sprinkle the chicken with the thyme and marjoram
3. Put the chicken in the air fryer basket. Surround with the

potatoes and drizzle the potatoes with the remaining olive oil mixture.
4. Roast for 25 minutes, and then test the temperature of the chicken. It should be 160°F. Test at the thickest part of the breast, making sure the probe does not touch bone. If the chicken is not done yet, return it to the air fryer and roast it for 4 to 5 minutes, or until the temperature is 160°F.
5. When the chicken is done, transfer it and the potatoes to a serving platter and cover with foil. Let the chicken rest for 5 minutes before serving.

Nutrition Info:

- Calories: 491 Fat: 13g Carbohydrates: 1g Protein: 2Sugar: 1gCholesterol: 170mg

Jerk Style Chicken Wings

Servings: 2-3 | Cooking Time: 25 Minutes

Ingredients:

- 1g ground thyme
- 1g dried rosemary
- 2g allspice
- 4g ground ginger
- 3 g garlic powder
- 2g onion powder
- 1g of cinnamon
- 2g of paprika
- 2g chili powder
- 1g nutmeg
- Salt to taste
- 30 ml of vegetable oil
- 0.5 - 1 kg of chicken wings
- 1 lime, juice

Directions:

1. Select Preheat, set the temperature to 200°C and press Start/Pause.
2. Combine all spices and oil in a bowl to create a marinade.
3. Mix the chicken wings in the marinade until they are well covered.
4. Place the chicken wings in the preheated air fryer.
5. Select Chicken and press Start/Pause. Be sure to shake the baskets in the middle of cooking.
6. Remove the wings and place them on a serving plate.
7. Squeeze fresh lemon juice over the wings and serve.

Nutrition Info:

- Calories: 240 Fat: 15gCarbohydrate: 5g Protein: 19g Sugars: 4g Cholesterol: 60mg

Air Fried Maple Chicken Thighs

Servings: 4 | Cooking Time:25minutes

Ingredients:

- One egg
- Buttermilk: 1 cup
- Maple syrup: half cup
- Chicken thighs: 4 pieces
- Granulated garlic: 1 tsp.
- Dry Mix
- Granulated garlic: half tsp.
- All-purpose flour: half cup
- Salt: one tbsp.
- Sweet paprika: one tsp.
- Smoked paprika: half tsp.
- Tapioca flour: ¼ cup
- Cayenne pepper: ¼ teaspoon
- Granulated onion: one tsp.
- Black pepper: ¼ teaspoon
- Honey powder: half tsp.

Directions:

1. In a ziploc bag, add egg, one tsp. of granulated garlic, buttermilk, and maple syrup, add in the chicken thighs and let it marinate for one hour or more in the refrigerator
2. In a mixing bowl, add sweet paprika, tapioca flour, granulated onion, half tsp. of granulated garlic, flour, cayenne pepper, salt, pepper, honey powder, and smoked paprika mix it well.
3. Let the air fry preheat to 380 F
4. Coat the marinated chicken thighs in the dry spice mix, shake the excess off.
5. Put the chicken skin side down in the air fryer
6. Let it cook for 12 minutes. Flip thighs halfway through and cook for 13 minutes more.
7. Serve with salad greens.

Nutrition Info:

- 415.4 calories| protein 23.3g| carbohydrates 20.8g| fat 13.4g

Breaded Chicken Tenderloins

Servings: 4 | Cooking Time:12 Minutes

Ingredients:

- Eight chicken tenderloins
- Olive oil: 2 tablespoons
- One egg whisked
- 1/4 cup breadcrumbs

Directions:

1. Let the air fryer heat to 180 C.
2. In a big bowl, add breadcrumbs and oil, mix well until forms a crumbly mixture
3. Dip chicken tenderloin in whisked egg and coat in breadcrumbs mixture.
4. Place the breaded chicken in the air fryer and cook at 180C for 12 minutes or more.
5. Take out from the air fryer and serve with your favorite green salad.

Nutrition Info:

- Calories 206|Proteins 20g |Carbs 17g |Fat 10g |

Ginger Chili Broccoli

Servings: 5 | Cooking Time: 25 Minutes

Ingredients:

- 8 cups broccoli florets
- 1/2 cup olive oil
- 2 fresh lime juice
- 2 tbsp fresh ginger, grated
- 2 tsp chili pepper, chopped

Directions:

1. Add broccoli florets into the steamer and steam for 8 minutes.
2. Meanwhile, for dressing in a small bowl, combine lime-juice, oil, ginger, and chili pepper.
3. Add steamed broccoli in a large bowl then pour dressing over broccoli. Toss well.

Nutrition Info:

- Calories 239 Fat 20.8 g, Carbohydrates 13.7 g, Sugar 3 g, Protein 4.5 g, Cholesterol 0 mg

Bell Peppers Frittata

Servings: 4 | Cooking Time: 20 Min

Ingredients:

- 2 Tablespoons olive oil
- 2 cups chicken sausage, casings removed and chopped
- One sweet onion, chopped
- 1 red bell pepper, chopped
- 1 orange bell pepper, chopped
- 1 green bell pepper, chopped
- Salt and black pepper to taste
- 8 eggs, whisked
- ½ cup mozzarella cheese, shredded
- 2 teaspoons oregano, chopped

Directions:

1. Add 1 spoonful of oil to the air fryer, add bacon, heat to 320 degrees F, and brown for 1 minute.
2. Remove remaining butter, onion, red bell pepper, orange and white, mix and simmer for another 2 minutes.
3. Stir and cook for 15 minutes, add oregano, salt, pepper, and eggs.
4. Add mozzarella, leave frittata aside for a couple of minutes, divide and serve between plates.
5. Enjoy.

Nutrition Info:

- calories 212, fat 4g, fiber 6g, carbs 8g, protein 12g

Lemon Pepper Chicken Breast

Servings: 2 | Cooking Time:15 Minutes

Ingredients:

- Two Lemons rind, juice, and zest
- One Chicken Breast
- Minced Garlic: 1 Tsp
- Black Peppercorns: 2 tbsp.
- Chicken Seasoning: 1 Tbsp.
- Salt & pepper, to taste

Directions:

1. Let the air fryer preheat to 180C.
2. In a large aluminum foil, add all the seasonings along with lemon rind.
3. Add salt and pepper to chicken and rub the seasonings all over chicken breast.
4. Put the chicken in aluminum foil. And fold it tightly.
5. Flatten the chicken inside foil with a rolling pin
6. Put it in the air fryer and cook at 180 C for 15 minutes.
7. Serve hot.

Nutrition Info:

- Calories: 140 | Carbohydrates: 24g | Protein: 13g | Fat: 2g

Dry Rub Chicken Wings

Servings: 4 | Cooking Time: 30 Minutes

Ingredients:

- 9g garlic powder
- 1 cube of chicken broth, reduced sodium
- 5g of salt
- 3g black pepper
- 1g smoked paprika
- 1g cayenne pepper
- 3g Old Bay seasoning, sodium free
- 3g onion powder
- 1g dried oregano
- 453g chicken wings
- Nonstick Spray Oil
- Ranch sauce, to serve

Directions:

1. Preheat the air fryer. Set the temperature to 180 °C.
2. Put ingredients in a bowl and mix well.
3. Season the chicken wings with half the seasoning mixture and sprinkle abundantly with oil spray.
4. Place the chicken wings in the preheated air fryer.
5. Select Chicken, set the timer to 30 minutes.
6. Shake the baskets halfway through cooking.
7. Transfer the chicken wings to a bowl and sprinkle them with the other half of the seasonings until they are well covered. Serve with ranch sauce

Nutrition Info:

- Calories: 89 Fat: 6.33gCarbohydrates: 0g Protein: 7.56g Sugar: 0g

Pork Tenderloin With Mustard Glazed

Servings: 4 | Cooking Time:18 Minutes

Ingredients:

- Yellow mustard: ¼ cup
- One pork tenderloin
- Salt: ¼ tsp
- Honey: 3 Tbsp.
- Freshly ground black pepper: ⅛ tsp
- Minced garlic: 1 Tbsp.
- Dried rosemary: 1 tsp
- Italian seasoning: 1 tsp

Directions:

1. With a knife, cut the top of pork tenderloin. Add garlic (minced) in the cuts. Then sprinkle with kosher salt and pepper.
2. In a bowl, add honey, mustard, rosemary, and Italian seasoning mix until combined. Rub this mustard mix all over pork.
3. Let it marinate in the refrigerator for at least two hours.
4. Put pork tenderloin in the air fryer basket. Cook for 18-20 minutes at 400 F. with an instant-read thermometer internal temperature of pork should be 145 F
5. Take out from the air fryer and serve with a side of salad.

Nutrition Info:

- Calories: 390 | Carbohydrates: 11g | Protein: 59g | Fat: 11g |

Air Fryer Hen Wings

Servings: 4 | Cooking Time: 15 Minutes

Ingredients:

- 6 Chicken Wings - Flats and Drumettes
- Olive Oil Spray
- Salt
- Pepper
- Barbecue Sauce

Directions:

1. Splash the air fryer basket or foil-lined air fryer basket with non-stick cooking spray.
2. Arrange the wings equally into the basket. In a 4-quart air fryer basket, 6 wings fit well. Readjust this as required for the dimension of your air fryer.
3. Include an even layer of olive oil spray, a dashboard of salt, and pepper to the wings.
4. Prepare at 390° for 10 minutes.
5. Turn and also cook for an extra 10 minutes at 390 levels.
6. Make certain the internal temperature of the wings goes to the very least 165°.
7. Coat with BBQ sauce if you prefer or other dipping sauces.

Nutrition Info:

- Calories: 308 kcal; Protein:17 g; Fat:11 g; Carbs: 0g

Chicken Bites In Air Fryer

Servings: 3 | Cooking Time:10 Minutes

Ingredients:

- Chicken breast: 2 cups
- Kosher salt& pepper to taste
- Smashed potatoes: one cup
- Scallions: ¼ cup
- One Egg beat
- Whole wheat breadcrumbs: 1 cup

Directions:

1. Boil the chicken until soft.
2. Shred the chicken with the help of a fork.
3. Add the smashed potatoes, scallions to the shredded chicken. Season with kosher salt and pepper.
4. Coat with egg and then in bread crumbs.
5. Put in the air fryer, and cook for 8 minutes at 380F. Or until golden brown.
6. Serve warm.

Nutrition Info:

- Calories: 234|protein 25g| carbs 15g|fat 9 g

Air Fryer Chicken Cheese Quesadilla

Servings: 3 | Cooking Time: 6 Minutes

Ingredients:

- 2 flour tortillas.
- 1 cup precooked hen diced.
- 1 mug shredded cheese.

Directions:

1. Set one flour tortilla into the air fryer. Add in cheese and chicken. Spread equally.
2. Top with the second tortilla. Place a metal shelf on the top to keep it from moving.
3. Prepare at 370F for 6 mins, flipping half means.
4. Cut and also serve.

Nutrition Info:

- Calories: 171 kcal; Carbs: 8 g; Protein: 15g; Fat: 8 g.

Rotisserie Chicken

Servings: 2 | Cooking Time: 30 Minutes

Ingredients:

- 1 Whole chicken
- 2 tbsps. ghee
- 1 tbsp. magic mushroom powder
- Salt

Directions:

1. Preheat the Air Fryer to 3700F. Merge ghee and magic mushroom powder in a small mixing bowl.
2. Pull back the skin on the chicken breast and scoop some of the ghee mixture between the breast and skin with a spoon.

3. Push the mixture with your fingers. Repeat this for the other breast. Season the chicken with salt.
4. Put the chicken breast-side down onto the wire basket. Cook at 3650 F for about 30 minutes.
5. Serve.

Nutrition Info:

- Calories: 226 kcal; Carbs: 0g; Fat: 14g; Proteins: 44g

Pork Dumplings In Air Fryer

Servings: 6 | Cooking Time:20 Minutes

Ingredients:

- 18 dumpling wrappers
- One teaspoon olive oil
- Bok choy: 4 cups (chopped)
- Rice vinegar: 2 tablespoons
- Diced ginger: 1 tablespoon
- Crushed red pepper: 1/4 teaspoon
- Diced garlic: 1 tablespoon
- Lean ground pork: half cup
- Cooking spray
- Lite soy sauce: 2 teaspoons
- Honey: half tsp.
- Toasted sesame oil: 1 teaspoon
- Finely chopped scallions

Directions:

1. In a large skillet, heat olive oil, add bok choy, cook for 6 minutes, and add garlic, ginger, and cook for one minute. Move this mixture on a paper towel and pat dry the excess oil
2. In a bowl, add bok choy mixture, crushed red pepper, and lean ground pork and mix well.
3. Lay a dumpling wrapper on a plate and add one tbsp. of filling in the wrapper's middle. With water, seal the edges and crimp it.
4. Air spray the air fryer basket, add dumplings in the air fryer basket and cook at 375 F for 12 minutes or until browned.
5. In the meantime, to make the sauce, add sesame oil, rice vinegar, scallions, soy sauce, and honey in a bowl mix together.
6. Serve the dumplings with sauce.

Nutrition Info:

- Calories 140| Fat 5g |Protein 12g |Carbohydrate 9g|

Tasty Chicken Tenders

Servings: 4 | Cooking Time: 25 Minutes

Ingredients:

- 1 ½ lbs chicken tenders
- 1 tbsp. extra virgin olive oil
- 1 tsp. rotisserie chicken seasoning
- 2 tbsp. BBQ sauce

Directions:

1. Add all ingredients except oil in a zip-lock bag.
2. Seal bag and place in the refrigerator for 2-3 hours.
3. Heat oil in a large pan over medium heat.
4. Cook marinated chicken tenders in a pan until lightly brown and cooked.

Nutrition Info:

- Calories 365 Fat 16.1 g, Carbohydrates 2.8 g, Sugar 2 g, Protein 49.2 g, Cholesterol 151 mg

Buttermilk Fried Chicken

Servings: 4 | Cooking Time: 10 Minutes

Ingredients:

- 3 tablespoons cornmeal, ground
- 1-pound chicken breasts, pastured
- 6 tablespoons cornflakes
- 1 teaspoon garlic powder
- ¼ teaspoon ground black pepper
- 1 teaspoon paprika
- ¼ teaspoon salt
- ¼ teaspoon hot sauce
- 1/3 cup buttermilk, low-fat

Directions:

1. Pour milk in a bowl, add hot sauce and whisk until well mixed.
2. Cut the chicken in half lengthwise into four pieces, then add into buttermilk, toss well until well coated and let it sit for 15 minutes.
3. Place cornflakes in a blender or food processor, pulse until mixture resembles crumbs, then add remaining ingredients, pulse until well mixed and then tip the mixture into a shallow dish.
4. After 15 minutes, remove chicken from the buttermilk, then coat with cornflakes mixture until evenly coated and place the chicken on a wire rack.
5. Switch on the air fryer, insert fryer basket, grease it with olive oil, then shut with its lid, set the fryer at 375 degrees F and preheat for 5 minutes.
6. Then open the fryer, add chicken in it in a single layer, spray with oil, close with its lid and cook for 10 minutes until nicely golden and cooked, turning the chicken halfway through the frying.
7. When air fryer beeps, open its lid, transfer chicken onto a serving plate and serve.

Nutrition Info:

- Calories: 160 CalCarbs: 7 gFat: 3.5 gProtein: 24 gFiber: 1 g

Air Fryer Vegetables & Italian Sausage

Servings: 4 | Cooking Time:14 Minutes

Ingredients:

- One bell pepper
- Italian Sausage: 4 pieces spicy or sweet
- One small onion
- 1/4 cup of mushrooms

Directions:

1. Let the air fryer pre-heat to 400 F for three minutes.
2. Put Italian sausage in a single layer in the air fryer basket and let it cook for six minutes.
3. Slice the vegetables while the sausages are cooking.
4. After six minutes, reduce the temperature to 360 F. flip the sausage halfway through. Add the mushrooms, onions, and peppers in the basket around the sausage.
5. Cook at 360 F for 8 minutes. After a 4-minute mix around the sausage and vegetables.
6. With an instant-read thermometer, the sausage temperature should be 160 F.
7. Cook more for few minutes if the temperature is not 160F.
8. Take vegetables and sausage out and serve hot with brown rice.

Nutrition Info:

- calories 291| fat: 21g| carbs 10g|Protein: 16g

Chicken Thighs Smothered Style

Servings: 4 | Cooking Time:30 Minutes

Ingredients:

- 8-ounce of chicken thighs
- 1 tsp paprika
- One pinch salt
- Mushrooms: half cup
- Onions, roughly sliced

Directions:

1. Let the air fryer preheat to 400F
2. Chicken thighs season with paprika, salt, and pepper on both sides.
3. Place the thighs in the air fryer and cook for 20 minutes.
4. Meanwhile, sauté the mushroom and onion.
5. Take out the thighs from the air fryer serve with sautéed mushrooms and onions.
6. And serve with chopped scallions and on the side of salad greens

Nutrition Info:

- Kcal 466.3| Fat: 32g| Net Carbs: 2.4g|Protein: 40.5g

Chapter 5:
Beef, Pork And
Lamb Recipes

Chapter 5: Beef, Pork And Lamb Recipes

Apple Mini Cakes

Servings: 2 | Cooking Time: 10 Minutes

Ingredients:

- 1 medium apple, peeled and diced, into bite-sized pieces
- 18g granulated sugar
- 18g unsalted butter
- 2g ground cinnamon
- 1g ground nutmeg
- 1g ground allspice
- 1 sheet prefabricated cake dough
- 1 beaten egg
- 5 ml of milk

Directions:

1. Put diced apples, granulated sugar, butter, cinnamon, nutmeg, and allspice in a medium saucepan or in a skillet over medium-low heat.
2. Simmer for 2 minutes and remove from heat.
3. Allow the apples to cool, discovered at room temperature for 30 minutes.
4. Cut the cake dough into circles of 127 mm.
5. Add the filling to the center of each circle and use your finger to apply water to the outer ends. Some filler will be left unused.
6. Close the cake cut a small opening at the top.
7. Preheat the air fryer for a few minutes and set the temperature to 175°C.
8. Mix the eggs and milk and spread the mixture on each foot.
9. Place the cakes in the preheated air fryer and cook at 175°C for 10 minutes until the cakes are golden brown.

Nutrition Info:

- (Nutrition per Serving)Calories: 185 Fat: 11Carbohydrates: 38g Protein: 5g Sugar: 20g Cholesterol: 11mg

Meatloaf Reboot

Servings: 2 | Cooking Time: 9 Minutes

Ingredients:

- 4 slices of leftover meatloaf, cut about 1-inch thick.

Directions:

1. Preheat your air fryer to 350 degrees.
2. Spray each side of the meatloaf slices with cooking spray. Add the slices to the air fryer and cook for about 9 to 10 minutes. Don't turn the slices halfway through the cooking cycle, because they may break apart. Instead, keep them on one side to cook to ensure they stay together

Nutrition Info:

- Calories: 201 Fat: 5g Carbohydrates: 9.6g Protein: 38g Sugar: 1.8g Cholesterol: 10mg

Air Fryer Bacon

Servings: 4 | Cooking Time: 10 Minutes

Ingredients:

- 11 slices bacon

Directions:

1. Divide the bacon in half, and place the first half in the air fryer.
2. Set the temperature at 401 degrees F, and set the timer to 11 mins.
3. Check it halfway through to see if anything needs to be rearranged.
4. Cook remainder of the time. Serve.

Nutrition Info:

- Calories: 91 kcal / Carbs: 0g / Protein: 2g / Fat: 8g

Air Fried Empanadas

Servings: 2 | Cooking Time:20 Minutes

Ingredients:

- Square gyoza wrappers: eight pieces
- Olive oil: 1 tablespoon
- White onion: 1/4 cup, finely diced
- Mushrooms: 1/4 cup, finely diced
- Half cup lean ground beef
- Chopped garlic: 2 teaspoons
- Paprika: 1/4 teaspoon
- Ground cumin: 1/4 teaspoon
- Six green olives, diced
- Ground cinnamon: 1/8 teaspoon
- Diced tomatoes: half cup
- One egg, lightly beaten

Directions:

1. In a skillet, over a medium flame, add oil, onions, and beef and cook for 3 minutes, until beef turns brown.
2. Add mushrooms and cook for six minutes until it starts to brown. Then add paprika, cinnamon, olives, cumin, and garlic and cook for 3 minutes or more.
3. Add in the chopped tomatoes, and cook for a minute. Turn off the heat; let it cool for five minutes.
4. Lay gyoza wrappers on a flat surface add one and a half tbsp. of beef filling in each wrapper. Brush edges with water or egg, fold wrappers, pinch edges.
5. Put four empanadas in an even layer in an air fryer basket, and cook for 7 minutes at 400°F until nicely browned.
6. Serve with sauce and salad greens.

Nutrition Info:

- per serving Calories 343 |Fat 19g |Protein 18g |Carbohydrate 12.9g

Mustard-crusted Fish Fillets

Servings: 4 | Cooking Time: 8 To 11 Minutes

Ingredients:

- 5 teaspoons low-sodium yellow mustard (see Tip)
- 1 tablespoon freshly squeezed lemon juice
- 4 (3.5-ounce) sole fillets
- ½ teaspoon dried thyme
- ½ teaspoon dried marjoram
- ⅛ teaspoon freshly ground black pepper
- 1 slice low-sodium whole-wheat bread, crumbled
- 2 teaspoons olive oil

Directions:

1. In a small bowl, stir the mustard and lemon juice. Spread this evenly over the fillets. Place them in the air fryer basket.
2. In another small bowl, mix the thyme, marjoram, pepper, bread crumbs, and olive oil. Mix until combined.
3. Gently but firmly press the spice mixture onto the top of each fish fillet.
4. Bake for 8 to 11 minutes, or until the fish reaches an internal temperature of at least 145°F on a meat thermometer and the topping is browned and crisp. Serve immediately.

Nutrition Info:

- Calories: 142 Fat: 4g (25% of calories from fat) Saturated Fat: 1g Protein: 20g Carbohydrates: 5g Sodium: 140g Fiber: 1g Sugar: 1g; 4 DV vitamin C

Cranberry And Lemon Muffins

Servings:6-8 | Cooking Time: 15 Minutes

Ingredients:

- 5 ml of lemon juice
- 112g of coconut milk or soymilk
- 120g all-purpose flour
- 4g baking powder
- 2g of baking soda
- 1g of salt
- 50g granulated sugar
- 60 ml coconut oil, liquid
- 1 lemon, lemon zest
- 5 ml vanilla extract
- 75g of fresh blueberries
- Nonstick Spray Oil

Directions:

1. Put the lemon juice and coconut milk in a small bowl and then set the mixture aside. Mix the flour, baking powder, baking soda and salt in a separate bowl and set aside. Mix the sugar, coconut oil, lemon zest and vanilla extract in an additional bowl. Then, combine with the coconut-lemon mixture and stir to combine.
2. Mix the dry ingredients to the wet ones gradually, until the mixture is smooth. Gently place the blueberries.
3. Preheat the air fryer for 5 minutes and set the temperature to 150°C.
4. Grease the muffin molds with oil spray and pour the mixture until the cups are ¾.
5. Place the muffin molds carefully in the preheated air fryer. Set the timer to 15 minutes at 150°C.
6. Remove the muffins when you finish cooking and let them cool for 10 minutes. Then serve them.

Nutrition Info:

- Calories: 120 Fat: 0g Carbohydrates: 0g Protein: 0g Sugar: 0g Cholesterol: 12mg

Pumpkin Spice Snack Balls

Servings: 10 | Cooking Time: 10 Minutes

Ingredients:

- 1 ½ cups old-fashioned oats
- ½ cup chopped almonds
- ½ cup unsweetened shredded coconut
- ¾ cup canned pumpkin puree
- 2 tablespoons honey
- 2 teaspoons pumpkin pie spice
- ¼-teaspoon salt

Directions:

1. Preheat the oven to 300°F and line a baking sheet with parchment.
2. Combine the oats, almonds, and coconut on the baking sheet.
3. Bake for 8 to 10 minutes until browned, stirring halfway through.
4. Place the pumpkin, honey, pumpkin pie spice, and salt in a medium bowl.
5. Stir in the toasted oat mixture.
6. Shape the mixture into 20 balls by hand and place on a tray.
7. Chill until the balls are firm then serve.

Nutrition Info:

- Calories 170 Total Fat 0.7g, Saturated Fat 0.1g, Total Carbs 14.7g, Net Carbs 12.2g, Protein 2.1g, Sugar 2.2g, Fiber 2.5g, Sodium 1mg

Snapper With Fruit

Servings: 4 | Cooking Time: 9 To 13 Minutes

Ingredients:

- 4 (4-ounce) red snapper fillets
- 2 teaspoons olive oil
- 3 nectarines, halved and pitted
- 3 plums, halved and pitted
- 1 cup red grapes
- 1 tablespoon freshly squeezed lemon juice
- 1 tablespoon honey
- ½ teaspoon dried thyme

Directions:

1. Put the red snapper in the air fryer basket and drizzle

with the olive oil. Air-fry for 4 minutes.
2. Remove the basket and add the nectarines and plums. Scatter the grapes over all.
3. Drizzle with the lemon juice and honey and sprinkle with the thyme.
4. Put back the basket to the air fryer and air-fry for 5 to 9 minutes more, or until the fish flakes when tested with a fork and the fruit is tender. Serve immediately.

Nutrition Info:
• Calories: 245 Fat: 4g (15% of calories from fat) Saturated Fat: 1g Protein: 25g Carbohydrates: 28g Sodium: 73mg Fiber: 3g Sugar: 24g 11% DV vitamin A 27% DV vitamin C

Steak

Servings: 2 | Cooking Time: 18 Minutes

Ingredients:
• 2 steaks, grass-fed, each about 6 ounces and ¾ inch thick
• 1 tablespoon butter, unsalted
• ¾ teaspoon ground black pepper
• 1/2 teaspoon garlic powder
• ¾ teaspoon salt
• 1 teaspoon olive oil

Directions:
1. Switch on the air fryer, insert fryer basket, grease it with olive oil, then shut with its lid, set the fryer at 400 degrees F and preheat for 5 minutes.
2. Meanwhile, coat the steaks with oil and then season with black pepper, garlic, and salt.
3. Open the fryer, add steaks in it, close with its lid and cook 10 to 18 minutes at until nicely golden and steaks are cooked to desired doneness, flipping the steaks halfway through the frying.
4. When air fryer beeps, open its lid and transfer steaks to a cutting board.
5. Take two large pieces of aluminum foil, place a steak on each piece, top steak with ½ tablespoon butter, then cover with foil and let it rest for 5 minutes.
6. Serve straight away.

Nutrition Info:
• Calories: 82 CalCarbs: 0 gFat: 5 gProtein: 8.7 gFiber: 0 g

Beef Scallops

Servings: 4 | Cooking Time: 20 Minutes

Ingredients:
• 16 veal scallops
• Salt
• Ground pepper
• Garlic powder
• 2 eggs
• Breadcrumbs
• Extra virgin olive oil

Directions:

1. Put the beef scallops well spread, salt, and pepper. Add some garlic powder.
2. In a bowl, beat the eggs.
3. In another bowl put the breadcrumbs.
4. Pass the Beef scallops for beaten egg and then for the breadcrumbs.
5. Spray with extra virgin olive oil on both sides.
6. Put a batch in the basket of the air fryer. Do not pile the scallops too much.
7. Select 1800C, 15 minutes. From time to time, shake the basket so that the scallops move.
8. When finishing that batch, put the next one and so on until you finish with everyone, usually 4 or 5 scallops enter per batch.

Nutrition Info:
• Calories: 330 Fat: 3.41g Carbohydrates: 0g Protein: 20.99g Sugar: 0g Cholesterol:1 65mg

Homemade Muffins

Servings: 3 | Cooking Time: 15 Minutes

Ingredients:
• 6 tbsp. olive oil
• 100g of sugar
• 2 eggs
• 100g flour
• 1 tsp. Royal baking powder
• Lemon zest

Directions:
1. Beat the eggs with the sugar, with the help of a whisk. Add the oil little by little, while stirring, until you get a fluffy cream.
2. Then add the lemon zest.
3. Finally, add the sifted flour with the yeast to the previous mixture and mix in an envelope.
4. Fill 2/3 of the muffin muffins with the dough.
5. Preheat the air fryer a few minutes to 1800C and when ready place the muffins in the basket.
6. Set the timer for approximately 20 minutes at a temperature of 1800C, until they are golden brown.

Nutrition Info:
• Calories: 240 Fat: 12g Carbohydrates: 29g Protein: 4g Sugar: 100g Cholesterol: 67g

Marinated Loin Potatoes

Servings: 2 | Cooking Time: 1h

Ingredients:
• 2 medium potatoes
• 4 fillets of marinated loin
• A little extra virgin olive oil
• Salt

Directions:
1. Peel the potatoes and cut. Cut with match-sized mando-

lin, potatoes with a cane but very thin.
2. Wash and immerse in water 30 minutes.
3. Drain and dry well.
4. Add a little oil and stir so that the oil permeates well in all the potatoes.
5. Go to the basket of the air fryer and distribute well.
6. Cook at 1600C for 10 minutes.
7. Take out the basket, shake so that the potatoes take off. Let the potato tender. If it is not, leave 5 more minutes.
8. Place the steaks on top of the potatoes.
9. Select, 10 minutes, and 1800C for 5 minutes again.

Nutrition Info:

• Calories: 136 kcal; Fat: 5.1g; Carbs: 1.9g; Protein: 20.7g

Pork Trinoza Wrapped In Ham

Servings: 6 | Cooking Time: 20 Minutes

Ingredients:

• 6 pieces of Serrano ham, thinly sliced
• 454g pork, halved, with butter and crushed
• 6g of salt
• 1g black pepper
• 227g fresh spinach leaves, divided
• 4 slices of mozzarella cheese, divided
• 18g sun-dried tomatoes, divided
• 10 ml of olive oil, divided

Directions:

1. Place 3 pieces of ham on baking paper, slightly overlapping each other. Place 1 half of the pork in the ham. Repeat with the other half.
2. Season the inside of the pork rolls with salt and pepper.
3. Place half of the spinach, cheese, and sun-dried tomatoes on top of the pork loin, leaving a 13 mm border on all sides.
4. Roll the fillet around the filling well and tie with a kitchen cord to keep it closed.
5. Repeat the process for the other pork steak and place them in the fridge.
6. Select Preheat in the air fryer and press Start/Pause.
7. Brush 5 ml of olive oil on each wrapped steak and place them in the preheated air fryer.
8. Select Steak. Set the timer to 9 minutes and press Start/Pause.
9. Allow it to cool for 10 minutes before cutting.

Nutrition Info:

• Calories: 282 Fat: 23.41 Carbohydrates: 0g Protein: 16.59 Sugar: 0g Cholesterol: 73gm

Grain-free Berry Cobbler

Servings: 10 | Cooking Time: 25 Minutes

Ingredients:

• 4 cups fresh mixed berries
• ½-cup ground flaxseed
• ¼ cup almond meal
• ¼ cup unsweetened shredded coconut
• ½-tablespoon baking powder
• 1-teaspoon ground cinnamon
• ¼-teaspoon salt
• Powdered stevia, to taste
• 6 tablespoons coconut oil

Directions:

1. Preheat the oven to 375°F and lightly grease a 10-inch cast-iron skillet.
2. Spread the berries on the bottom of the skillet.
3. Whisk together the dry ingredients in a mixing bowl.
4. Cut in the coconut oil using a fork to create a crumbled mixture.
5. Spread the crumble over the berries and bake for 25 minutes until hot and bubbling.
6. Cool the cobbler for 5 to 10 minutes before serving.

Nutrition Info:

• Calories 215,Total Fat 13.6gSaturated Fat 1.2g, Total Carbs 5.3g, Net Carbs 2.2g, Protein 5g, Sugar 1g,Fiber 3.1g, Sodium 67mg

Roasted Pork

Servings: 2-4 | Cooking Time: 30 Minutes

Ingredients:

• 500-2000g Pork meat (To roast)
• Salt
• Oil

Directions:

1. Join the cuts in an orderly manner.
2. Place the meat on the plate
3. Varnish with a little oil.
4. Place the roasts with the fat side down.
5. Cook in air fryer at 1800C for 30 minutes.
6. Turn when you hear the beep.
7. Remove from the oven. Drain excess juice.
8. Let stand for 10 minutes on aluminum foil before serving.

Nutrition Info:

• Calories: 820 Fat: 41g Carbohydrates: 0g Protein: 20.99g Sugar: 0g Cholesterol: 120mg

Air Fryer Beef Steak Kabobs With Vegetables

Servings: 4 | Cooking Time:10 Minutes

Ingredients:

- Light Soy sauce: 2 tbsp.
- Lean beef chuck ribs: 4 cups, cut into one-inch pieces
- Low-fat sour cream: 1/3 cup
- Half onion
- 8 skewers: 6 inch
- One bell peppers

Directions:

1. In a mixing bowl, add soy sauce and sour cream, mix well. Add the lean beef chunks, coat well, and let it marinate for half an hour or more.
2. Cut onion, bell pepper into one-inch pieces. In water, soak skewers for ten minutes.
3. Add onions, bell peppers, and beef on skewers; alternatively, sprinkle with Black Pepper
4. Let it cook for 10 minutes in a preheated air fryer at 400F, flip halfway through.
5. Serve with yogurt dipping sauce.

Nutrition Info:

- Calories 268 |Proteins 20g |Carbs 15g|Fat 10g |

North Carolina Style Pork Chops

Servings: 2 | Cooking Time: 10 Minutes

Ingredients:

- 2 boneless pork chops
- 15 ml of vegetable oil
- 25g dark brown sugar, packaged
- 6g of Hungarian paprika
- 2g ground mustard
- 2g freshly ground black pepper
- 3g onion powder
- 3g garlic powder
- Salt and pepper to taste

Directions:

1. Preheat the air fryer a few minutes at 1800C.
2. Cover the pork chops with oil.
3. Put all the spices and season the pork chops abundantly, almost as if you were making them breaded.
4. Place the pork chops in the preheated air fryer.
5. Select Steak, set the time to 10 minutes.
6. Remove the pork chops when it has finished cooking. Let it stand for 5 minutes and serve.

Nutrition Info:

- Calories: 118 Fat: 6.85g Carbohydrates: 0 Protein: 13.12g Sugar: 0g Cholesterol: 39mg

Warm Chicken And Spinach Salad

Servings: 4 | Cooking Time: 16 To 20 Minutes

Ingredients:

- 3 (5-ounce) low-sodium boneless skinless chicken breasts, cut into 1-inch cubes
- 5 teaspoons olive oil
- ½ teaspoon dried thyme
- 1 medium red onion, sliced
- 1 red bell pepper, sliced
- 1 small zucchini, cut into strips
- 3 tablespoons freshly squeezed lemon juice
- 6 cups fresh baby spinach

Directions:

1. In a large bowl, mix the chicken with the olive oil and thyme. Toss to coat. Transfer to a medium metal bowl and roast for 8 minutes in the air fryer.
2. Add the red onion, red bell pepper, and zucchini. Roast for 8 to 12 minutes more, stirring once during cooking, or until the chicken reaches an internal temperature of 165°F on a meat thermometer.
3. Remove the bowl from the air fryer and stir in the lemon juice.
4. Put the spinach in a serving bowl and top with the chicken mixture. Toss to combine and serve immediately.

Nutrition Info:

- Calories: 214 Fat: 7g (29% of calories from fat) Saturated Fat: 1g Protein: 28g Carbohydrates: 7g Sodium: 116mg Fiber: 2g Sugar: 4g 90% DV vitamin A 69% DV vitamin C

Double Cheeseburger

Servings: 1 | Cooking Time: 18 Minutes

Ingredients:

- 2 beef patties, pastured
- 1/8 teaspoon onion powder
- 2 slices of mozzarella cheese, low fat
- 1/8 teaspoon ground black pepper
- 1/8 teaspoon salt

Directions:

1. Switch on the air fryer, insert fryer basket, grease it with olive oil, then shut with its lid, set the fryer at 370 degrees F and preheat for 5 minutes.
2. Meanwhile, season the patties well with onion powder, black pepper, and salt.
3. Open the fryer, add beef patties in it, close with its lid and cook for 12 minutes until nicely golden and cooked, flipping the patties halfway through the frying.
4. Then top the patties with a cheese slice and continue cooking for 1 minute or until cheese melts.
5. Serve straight away.

Nutrition Info:

- Calories: 670 CalCarbs: 0 gFat: 50 gProtein: 39 gFiber: 0 g

Tex-mex Salmon Stir-fry

Servings: 4 | Cooking Time: 9 To 14 Minutes

Ingredients:

- 12 ounces salmon fillets, cut into 1½-inch cubes (see Tip)
- 1 red bell pepper, chopped
- 1 red onion, chopped
- 1 jalapeño pepper, minced
- ¼ cup low-sodium salsa
- 2 tablespoons low-sodium tomato juice
- 2 teaspoons peanut oil or safflower oil
- 1 teaspoon chili powder
- Brown rice or polenta, cooked (optional)

Directions:

1. In a medium bowl, mix together the salmon, red bell pepper, red onion, jalapeño, salsa, tomato juice, peanut oil, and chili powder.
2. Place the bowl in the air fryer and cook for 9 to 14 minutes, until the salmon is just cooked through and firm and the vegetables are crisp-tender, stirring once. Serve immediately over hot cooked brown rice or polenta, if desired.

Nutrition Info:

- Calories: 116 Fat: 3g (23% of calories from fat) Saturated Fat: 0g Protein: 18g Carbohydrates: 5g Sodium: 136mg Fiber: 0g Sugar: 3g 22% DV vitamin A 96% DV vitamin C

Strawberry Lime Pudding

Servings: 4 | Cooking Time: 10 Minutes

Ingredients:

- 2 cups plus 2 tablespoons fat-free milk
- 2 teaspoons flavorless gelatin
- 10 large strawberries, sliced
- 1-tablespoon fresh lime zest
- 2 teaspoons vanilla extract
- Liquid stevia extract, to taste

Directions:

1. Whisk together 2 tablespoons milk and gelatin in a medium bowl until the gelatin dissolves completely.
2. Place the strawberries in a food processor with the lime-juice and vanilla extract.
3. Blend until smooth then pour into a medium bowl.
4. Warm the remaining milk in a small saucepan over medium heat.
5. Stir in the lime zest and heat until steaming (do not boil).
6. Gently whisk the gelatin mixture into the hot milk then stir in the strawberry mixture.
7. Sweeten with liquid stevia to taste and chill until set. Serve cold.

Nutrition Info:

- Calories 70Total Fat 0.7g, Saturated Fat 0.1g, Total Carbs 14.7g, Net Carbs 12.2g, Protein 2.1g, Sugar 2.2g, Fiber 2.5g, Sodium 1mg

Pork On A Blanket

Servings: 4 | Cooking Time: 10 Minutes

Ingredients:

- 1/2 puff defrosted pastry sheet
- 16 thick smoked sausages
- 15 ml of milk

Directions:

1. Adjust the temperature of the air fryer to 200°C and set the timer to 5 minutes.
2. Cut the puff pastry into 64 x 38 mm strips.
3. Place a cocktail sausage at the end of the puff pastry and roll around the sausage, sealing the dough with some water.
4. Brush the top of the sausages wrapped in milk and place them in the preheated air fryer.
5. Cook at 200°C for 10 minutes or until golden brown.

Nutrition Info:

- Calories: 242 kcal; Fat: 14g; Carbs: 0g; Protein: 27g

Roasted Vegetable Chicken Salad

Servings: 4 | Cooking Time: 10 To 13 Minutes

Ingredients:

- 3 (4-ounce) low-sodium boneless skinless chicken breasts, cut into 1-inch cubes (see Tip)
- 1 small red onion, sliced
- 1 red bell pepper, sliced
- 1 cup green beans, cut into 1-inch pieces
- 2 tablespoons low-fat ranch salad dressing
- 2 tablespoons freshly squeezed lemon juice
- ½ teaspoon dried basil
- 4 cups mixed lettuce

Directions:

1. In the air fryer basket, roast the chicken, red onion, red bell pepper, and green beans for 10 to 13 minutes, or until the chicken reaches an internal temperature of 165°F on a meat thermometer, tossing the food in the basket once during cooking.
2. While the chicken cooks, in a serving bowl, mix the ranch dressing, lemon juice, and basil.
3. Put the chicken and vegetables to a serving bowl and toss with the dressing to coat. Serve immediately on lettuce leaves.

Nutrition Info:

- Calories: 113 Fat: 1g (8% of calories from fat) Saturated Fat: 0g Protein: 19g Carbohydrates: 7g Sodium: 138g Fiber: 2g Sugar: 3g 13% DV vitamin A 42% DV vitamin C

Pork Fillets With Serrano Ham

Servings: 4 | Cooking Time: 20 Minutes

Ingredients:

- 400g of very thin sliced pork fillets
- 2 boiled and chopped eggs
- 100g chopped Serrano ham
- 1 beaten egg
- Breadcrumbs

Directions:

1. Make a roll with the pork fillets. Introduce half-cooked egg and Serrano ham. So that the roll does not lose its shape, fasten with a string or chopsticks.
2. Pass the rolls through the beaten egg and then through the breadcrumbs until it forms a good layer.
3. Adjust the temperature of the air fryer for a few minutes at 180° C.
4. Insert the rolls in the basket and set the timer for about 8 minutes at 180º C.
5. Serve.

Nutrition Info:

- Calories: 424 kcal; Fat: 15.15g; Carbs: 37.47g; Protein: 31.84g

Salmon On Bed Of Fennel And Carrot

Servings: 2 | Cooking Time: 13 To 14 Minutes

Ingredients:

- 1 fennel bulb, thinly sliced
- 1 large carrot, peeled and sliced
- 1 small onion, thinly sliced
- ¼ cup low-fat sour cream
- ¼ teaspoon coarsely ground pepper
- 2 (5 ounce) salmon fillets

Directions:

1. Combine the fennel, carrot, and onion in a bowl and toss.
2. Put the vegetable mixture into a 6-inch metal pan. Roast in the air fryer for 4 minutes or until the vegetables are crisp tender.
3. Remove the pan from the air fryer. Stir in the sour cream and sprinkle the vegetables with the pepper.
4. Top with the salmon fillets.
5. Return the pan to the air fryer. Roast for another 9 to 10 minutes or until the salmon just barely flakes when tested with a fork.

Nutrition Info:

- Calories: 253 Fat 9g (32% calories from fat) Saturated Fat: 1g Protein: 31g Carbohydrates: 12g Sodium: 115mg Fiber 3g Sugar: 5g 130% DV vitamin A 15% DV vitamin C

Air Fryer Steak

Servings: 2 | Cooking Time: 15 Minutes

Ingredients:

- 1 Ribeye Steak or New York City Strip Steak
- Salt and Pepper
- Garlic Powder
- Paprika
- Butter

Directions:

1. Place the meat to sit in a bowl at room temperature level.
2. Spray the olive oil onto both sides of the steak.
3. Add salt and pepper to season.
4. Add the garlic powder and paprika to the mixture.
5. Adjust the temperature of the air fryer to 400F.
6. Place steak in the air fryer and cook for 12 minutes flipping it halfway through.
7. Lead it with butter when ready, then serve.

Nutrition Info:

- Calories: 301 kcal; Fat: 23g; Carbs: 0g; Protein: 23g

Salmon Spring Rolls

Servings: 4 | Cooking Time: 8 To 10 Minutes

Ingredients:

- ½ pound salmon fillet
- 1 teaspoon toasted sesame oil
- 1 onion, sliced
- 8 rice paper wrappers
- 1 yellow bell pepper, thinly sliced
- 1 carrot, shredded
- ⅓ cup chopped fresh flat-leaf parsley
- ¼ cup chopped fresh basil

Directions:

1. Put the salmon in the air fryer basket and drizzle with the sesame oil. Add the onion. Air-fry for 8 to 10 minutes, or until the salmon just flakes when tested with a fork and the onion is tender.
2. Meanwhile, fill a small shallow bowl with warm water. One at a time, dip the rice paper wrappers into the water and place on a work surface.
3. Top each wrapper with one-eighth each of the salmon and onion mixture, yellow bell pepper, carrot, parsley, and basil. Roll up the wrapper, folding in the sides, to enclose the ingredients.
4. If you like, bake in the air fryer at 380°F for 7 to 9 minutes, until the rolls are crunchy. Cut the rolls in half to serve.

Nutrition Info:

- Calories: 95 Fat: 2g (19% of calories from fat) Saturated Fat: 0g Protein: 13g Carbohydrates: 8g Sodium: 98mg Fiber: 2g Sugar: 2g 73% DV vitamin A 158% DV vitamin C

Beef With Sesame And Ginger

Servings: 4-6 | Cooking Time: 23 Minutes

Ingredients:

- ½ cup tamari or soy sauce
- 3 tbsp. olive oil
- 2 tbsp. toasted sesame oil
- 1 tbsp. brown sugar
- 1 tbsp. ground fresh ginger
- 3 cloves garlic, minced
- 1 to 1½ pounds skirt steak, boneless sirloin, or low loin

Directions:

1. Put together the tamari sauce, oils, brown sugar, ginger, and garlic in small bowl. Add beef to a quarter-size plastic bag and pour the marinade into the bag. Press on the bag as much air as possible and seal it.
2. Refrigerate for 1 to 1½ hours, turning half the time. Remove the meat from the marinade and discard the marinade. Dry the meat with paper towels. Cook at a temperature of 350°F for 20 to 23 minutes, turning halfway through cooking.

Nutrition Info:

- Calories: 381 Fat: 5g Carbohydrates: 9.6g Protein: 38g Sugar: 1.8g Cholesterol: 0mg

Scallops With Green Vegetables

Servings: 4 | Cooking Time: 8 To 11 Minutes

Ingredients:

- 1 cup green beans
- 1 cup frozen peas
- 1 cup frozen chopped broccoli
- 2 teaspoons olive oil
- ½ teaspoon dried basil
- ½ teaspoon dried oregano
- 12 ounces sea scallops

Directions:

1. In a large bowl, toss the green beans, peas, and broccoli with the olive oil. Place in the air fryer basket. Air-fry for 4 to 6 minutes, or until the vegetables are crisp-tender.
2. Remove the vegetables from the air fryer basket and sprinkle with the herbs. Set aside.
3. In the air fryer basket, put the scallops and air-fry for 4 to 5 minutes, or until the scallops are firm and reach an internal temperature of just 145°F on a meat thermometer.
4. Toss scallops with the vegetables and serve immediately.

Nutrition Info:

- Calories: 124 Fat: 3g (22% of calories from fat) Saturated Fat: 0g Protein: 14g Carbohydrates: 11g Sodium: 56mg Fiber: 3g Sugar: 3g 15% DV vitamin A 46% DV vitamin C

Rustic Pear Pie With Nuts

Servings: 4 | Cooking Time: 45 Minutes

Ingredients:

- Cake
- 100g all-purpose flour
- 1g of salt
- 12g granulated sugar
- 84g unsalted butter, cold, cut into 13 mm pieces
- 30 ml of water, frozen
- 1 egg, beaten
- 12g turbinated sugar
- Nonstick Spray Oil
- 20g of honey
- 5 ml of water
- Roasted nuts, chopped, to decorate
- Filling:
- 1 large pear, peeled, finely sliced
- 5g cornstarch
- 24g brown sugar
- 1g ground cinnamon
- A pinch salt

Directions:

1. Mix 90 g of flour, salt, and granulated sugar in a large bowl until well combined. Join the butter in the mixture using a pastry mixer or food processor until thick crumbs form. Add cold water and mix until it joins. Shape the dough into a bowl, cover with plastic and let cool in the refrigerator for 1 hour.
2. Mix the stuffing ingredients in a bowl until they are combined. Roll a roll through your cooled dough until it is 216 mm in diameter. Add 10 g of flour on top of the dough leaving 38 mm without flour. Place the pear slices in decorative circles superimposed on the floured part of the crust. Remove any remaining pear juice on the slices. Fold the edge over the filling.
3. Cover the edges with beaten eggs and sprinkle the sugar over the whole cake. Set aside
4. Preheat the air fryer set the temperature to 160°C. Spray the preheated air fryer with oil spray and place the cake inside. Set the time to 45 minutes at 1600C. Mix the honey and water and pass the mixture through the cake when you finish cooking.
5. Garnish with toasted chopped nuts.

Nutrition Info:

- Calories: 20 Fat: 0g Carbohydrates: 0g Protein: 0g Sugar: 0g Cholesterol: 0mg

Mini Apple Oat Muffins

Servings: 24 | Cooking Time: 25 Minutes

Ingredients:

- 1 ½ cups old-fashioned oats
- 1-teaspoon baking powder
- ½-teaspoon ground cinnamon
- ¼-teaspoon baking soda
- ¼-teaspoon salt
- ½ cup unsweetened applesauce
- ¼-cup light brown sugar
- 3 tablespoons canola oil
- 3 tablespoons water
- 1-teaspoon vanilla extract
- ½ cup slivered almonds

Directions:

1. Preheat the oven to 350°F and grease a mini muffin pan.
2. Place the oats in a food processor and pulse into a fine flour.
3. Add the baking powder, cinnamon, baking soda, and salt.
4. Pulse until well combined then add the applesauce, brown sugar, canola oil, water, and vanilla then blend smooth.
5. Fold in the almonds and spoon the mixture into the muffin pan.
6. Bake for 22 to 25 minutes until a knife inserted in the center comes out clean.
7. Cool the muffins for 5 minutes then turn out onto a wire rack.

Nutrition Info:

- Calories 70Total Fat 0.7g, Saturated Fat 0.1g, Total Carbs 14.7g, Net Carbs 12.2g, Protein 2.1g, Sugar 2.2g, Fiber 2.5g, Sodium 1mg

Cinnamon Toasted Almonds

Servings: 8 | Cooking Time: 25 Minutes

Ingredients:

- 2 cups whole almonds
- 1-tablespoon olive oil
- 1-teaspoon ground cinnamon
- ½-teaspoon salt

Directions:

1. Preheat the oven to 325°F and line a baking sheet with parchment.
2. Toss together the almonds, olive oil, cinnamon, and salt.
3. Spread the almonds on the baking sheet in a single layer.
4. Bake for 25 minutes, stirring several times, until toasted.

Nutrition Info:

- Calories 150,Total Fat 13.6gSaturated Fat 1.2g, Total Carbs 5.3g, Net Carbs 2.2g, Protein 5g, Sugar 1g,Fiber 3.1g, Sodium 148mg

Pork Head Chops With Vegetables

Servings: 2-4 | Cooking Time: 20 Minutes

Ingredients:

- 4 pork head chops
- 2 red tomatoes
- 1 large green pepper
- 4 mushrooms
- 1 onion
- 4 slices of cheese
- Salt
- Ground pepper
- Extra virgin olive oil

Directions:

1. Put the four chops on a plate and salt and pepper.
2. Put two of the chops in the air fryer basket.
3. Place tomato slices, cheese slices, pepper slices, onion slices and mushroom slices. Add some threads of oil.
4. Take the air fryer and select 1800C, 15 minutes.
5. Check that the meat is well made and take out.
6. Repeat the same operation with the other two pork chops.

Nutrition Info:

- Calories: 106 Fat: 3.41g Carbohydrates: 0g Protein: 20.99g Sugar: 0g Cholesterol: 0mg

Fruity Coconut Energy Balls

Servings: 18 | Cooking Time: None

Ingredients:

- 1 cup chopped almonds
- 1 cup dried figs
- ½ cup dried apricots, chopped
- ½ cup dried cranberries, unsweetened
- ½-teaspoon vanilla extract
- ¼-teaspoon ground cinnamon
- ½ cup shredded unsweetened coconut

Directions:

1. Place the almonds, figs, apricots, and cranberries in a food processor.
2. Pulse the mixture until finely chopped.
3. Add the vanilla extract and cinnamon then pulse to combine once more.
4. Roll the mixture into 18 small balls by hand.
5. Roll the balls in the shredded coconut and chill until firm.

Nutrition Info:

- Calories 100 Total Fat 0.7g, Saturated Fat 0.1g, Total Carbs 14.7g, Net Carbs 12.2g, Protein 2.1g, Sugar 2.2g, Fiber 2.5g, Sodium 1mg

Chocolate Chip Muffins

Servings: 6-8 | Cooking Time: 15 Minutes

Ingredients:

- 50g granulated sugar
- 125 ml of coconut milk or soymilk
- 60 ml coconut oil, liquid
- 5 ml vanilla extract
- 120g all-purpose flour
- 14g cocoa powder
- 4g baking powder
- 2g of baking soda
- A pinch of salt
- 85g chocolate chips
- 25g of pistachios, cracked (optional)
- Nonstick Spray Oil

Directions:

1. Put the sugar, coconut milk, coconut oil and vanilla extract in a small bowl, then set aside. Mix the flour, cocoa powder, baking powder, baking soda and salt in a separate bowl and set aside.
2. Mix the dry ingredients with the wet ingredients gradually, until smooth. Then join with the chocolate and pistachio.
3. Preheat the air fryer for a few minutes and set the temperature to 150°C. Grease the muffin pans with oil spray and pour the mixture until they are filled to ¾.
4. Place the muffin molds carefully in the preheated air fryer. Set the time to 15 minutes at 150°C.
5. Remove the muffins when finished cooking and let them cool for 10 minutes before serving.

Nutrition Info:

- Calories: 374 Fat: 17.31g Carbohydrates: 48.86g Protein: 9.41g Sugar: 7.73 Cholesterol: 45g

Air Fry Rib-eye Steak

Servings: 2 | Cooking Time: 14 Minutes

Ingredients:

- Lean rib eye steaks: 2 medium-sized
- Salt & freshly ground black pepper, to taste

Directions:

1. Let the air fry preheat at 400 F. pat dry steaks with paper towels.
2. Use any spice blend or just salt and pepper on steaks.
3. Generously on both sides of the steak.
4. Put steaks in the air fryer basket. Cook according to the rareness you want. Or cook for 14 minutes and flip after half time.
5. Take out from the air fryer and let it rest for about 5 minutes.
6. Serve with microgreen salad.

Nutrition Info:

- Calories: 470kcal | Protein: 45g | Fat: 31g | carbs: 23g

Homemade Flamingos

Servings: 4 | Cooking Time: 20 Minutes

Ingredients:

- 400g of very thin sliced pork fillets c / n
- 2 boiled and chopped eggs
- 100g chopped Serrano ham
- 1 beaten egg
- Breadcrumbs

Directions:

1. Make a roll with the pork fillets. Introduce half-cooked egg and Serrano ham. So that the roll does not lose its shape, fasten with a string or chopsticks.
2. Pass the rolls through beaten egg and then through the breadcrumbs until it forms a good layer.
3. Preheat the air fryer a few minutes at 180° C.
4. Insert the rolls in the basket and set the timer for about 8 minutes at 180o C.
5. Serve right away.

Nutrition Info:

- Calories: 482 Fat: 23.41 Carbohydrates: 0g Protein: 16.59 Sugar: 0g Cholesterol: 173gm

Fish And Vegetable Tacos

Servings: 4 | Cooking Time: 9 To 12 Minutes

Ingredients:

- 1 pound white fish fillets, such as sole or cod
- 2 teaspoons olive oil
- 3 tablespoons freshly squeezed lemon juice, divided
- 1½ cups chopped red cabbage
- 1 large carrot, grated
- ½ cup low-sodium salsa
- ⅓ cup low-fat Greek yogurt
- 4 soft low-sodium whole-wheat tortillas

Directions:

1. Scrub the fish with the olive oil and drizzle with 1 tablespoon of lemon juice. Fry in the air fryer basket for 9 to 12 minutes, or till the fish just flakes when tested with a fork.
2. For the meantime, in a medium bowl, stir together the remaining 2 tablespoons of lemon juice, the red cabbage, carrot, salsa, and yogurt.
3. Once the fish is cooked, remove it from the air fryer basket and break it up into large pieces.

Nutrition Info:

- Calories: 209 Fat: 3g (13% of calories from fat) Saturated Fat: 0g Protein: 18g Carbohydrates: 30g Sodium: 116mg Fiber: 1g Sugar: 4g 70% DV vitamin A 43% DV vitamin C

Air Fried Steak With Asparagus Bundles

Servings: 2 | Cooking Time:30 Minutes

Ingredients:

- Olive oil spray
- Flank steak (2 pounds)- cut into 6 pieces
- Kosher salt and black pepper
- Two cloves of minced garlic
- Asparagus: 4 cups
- Tamari sauce: half cup
- Three bell peppers: sliced thinly
- Beef broth: 1/3 cup
- 1 Tbsp. of unsalted butter
- Balsamic vinegar: 1/4 cup

Directions:

1. Sprinkle salt and pepper on steak and rub.
2. In a ziploc bag, add garlic and Tamari sauce, then add steak, toss well and seal the bag.
3. Let it marinate for one hour to overnight.
4. Equally, place bell peppers and asparagus in the center of the steak.
5. Roll the steak around the vegetables and secure well with toothpicks.
6. Preheat the air fryer.
7. Spray the steak with olive oil spray. And place steaks in the air fryer.
8. Cook for 15 minutes at 400 degrees or more till steaks are cooked
9. Take the steak out from the air fryer and let it rest for five minute
10. Remove steak bundles and allow them to rest for 5 minutes before serving/slicing.
11. In the meantime, add butter, balsamic vinegar, and broth over medium flame. Mix well and reduce it by half. Add salt and pepper to taste.
12. Pour over steaks right before serving.

Nutrition Info:

- Calories 471 |Proteins 29g |Carbs 20g |Fat 15g |

Potatoes With Loin And Cheese

Servings: 4 | Cooking Time: 30 Minutes

Ingredients:

- 1kg of potatoes
- 1 large onion
- 1 piece of roasted loin
- Extra virgin olive oil
- Salt
- Ground pepper
- Grated cheese

Directions:

1. Peel the potatoes, cut the cane, wash, and dry.
2. Put salt and add some threads of oil, we bind well.

3. Pass the potatoes to the basket of the air fryer and select 1800C, 20 minutes.
4. Meanwhile, in a pan, put some extra virgin olive oil, add the peeled onion, and cut into julienne.
5. When the onion is transparent, add the chopped loin.
6. Sauté well and pepper.
7. Put the potatoes on a baking sheet.
8. Add the onion with the loin.
9. Cover with a layer of grated cheese.
10. Bake a little until the cheese takes heat and melts.

Nutrition Info:

- Calories: 332 Fat: 3.41g Carbohydrates: 0g Protein: 20.99g Sugar: 0g Cholesterol: 0mg

Stuffed Chicken

Servings: 4 | Cooking Time: 30 Minutes

Ingredients:

- 2 chicken breasts
- 2 tomatoes
- 200 g basil
- 1 teaspoon black pepper
- 1 teaspoon cayenne pepper
- 100 g tomato juice
- 40 g goat cheese

Directions:

1. Make a "pocket" from chicken breasts and rub it with black pepper and cayenne pepper.
2. Slice tomatoes and chop basil.
3. Chop the goat cheese.
4. Combine all the ingredients together – it will be the filling for breasts.
5. Fill the chicken breasts with this mixture.
6. Take a needle and thread and sew "pockets".
7. Preheat the air fryer oven to 200 C. Put the chicken breasts in the tray and pour it with tomato juice.
8. Serve.

Nutrition Info:

- Caloric content - 312 kcal Proteins – 41.6 grams Fats – 13.4 grams Carbohydrates – 5.6 grams

Lighter Fish And Chips

Servings: 4 | Cooking Time: 11 To 15 Minutes (chips), 11 To 15 Minutes (cod Fillets)

Ingredients:

- 2 russet potatoes, peeled, thinly sliced, rinsed, and patted dry (see Tip)
- 1 egg white
- 1 tablespoon freshly squeezed lemon juice
- ⅓ cup ground almonds
- 2 slices low-sodium whole-wheat bread, finely crumbled
- ½ teaspoon dried basil
- 4 (4-ounce) cod fillets

Directions:

1. Preheat the oven to warm.
2. Put the potato slices in the air fryer basket and air-fry for 11 to 15 minutes, or until crisp and brown. With tongs, turn the fries twice during cooking.
3. Meanwhile, in a shallow bowl, beat the egg white and lemon juice until frothy.
4. On a plate, mix the almonds, bread crumbs, and basil.
5. Separately, dip the fillets into the egg white mixture and then into the almond–bread crumb mixture to coat. Place the coated fillets on a wire rack to dry while the fries cook.
6. When the potatoes are done, transfer them to a baking sheet and keep warm in the oven on low heat
7. Air-fry the fish in the air fryer basket for 10 to 14 minutes, or until the fish reaches an internal temperature of at least 140°F on a meat thermometer and the coating is browned and crisp. Serve immediately with the potatoes.

Nutrition Info:

• Calories: 247 Fat: 5g (18% of calories from fat) Saturated Fat: 0g Protein: 27g Carbohydrates: 25g Sodium: 131mg Fiber: 3g Sugar: 3g 23% DV vitamin C

Dark Chocolate Almond Yogurt Cups

Servings: 6 | Cooking Time: None

Ingredients:

• 3 cups plain nonfat Greek yogurt
• ½-teaspoon almond extract
• ¼-teaspoon liquid stevia extract (more to taste)
• 2 ounces 70% dark chocolate, chopped
• ½ cup slivered almonds

Directions:

1. Whisk together the yogurt, almond extract, and liquid stevia in a medium bowl.
2. Spoon the yogurt into four dessert cups.
3. Sprinkle with chopped chocolate and slivered almonds.

Nutrition Info:

• Calories 170Total Fat 0.7g, Saturated Fat 0.1g, Total Carbs 14.7g, Net Carbs 12.2g, Protein 2.1g, Sugar 2.2g, Fiber 2.5g, Sodium 41mg

Diet Boiled Ribs

Servings: 4 | Cooking Time: 30 Minutes

Ingredients:

• 400 g pork ribs
• 1 teaspoon black pepper
• 1 g bay leaf
• 1 teaspoon basil
• 1 white onion
• 1 carrot
• 1 teaspoon cumin
• 700 ml water

Directions:

1. Cut the ribs on the portions and sprinkle it with black pepper.
2. Take a big saucepan and pour water in it.
3. Add the ribs and bay leaf.
4. Peel the onion and carrot and add it to the water with meat.
5. Sprinkle it with cumin and basil.
6. Cook it on the medium heat in the air fryer for 30 minutes.

Nutrition Info:

• Caloric content – 294 kcal Proteins – 27.1 grams Fats – 17.9 grams Carbohydrates – 4.8 grams

Nutty Chicken Nuggets

Servings: 4 | Cooking Time: 10 To 13 Minutes

Ingredients:

• 1 egg white
• 1 tablespoon freshly squeezed lemon juice
• ½ teaspoon dried basil
• ½ teaspoon ground paprika
• 1 pound low-sodium boneless skinless chicken breasts, cut into 1½-inch cubes
• ½ cup ground almonds
• 2 slices low-sodium whole-wheat bread, crumbled

Directions:

1. In a shallow bowl, beat the egg white, lemon juice, basil, and paprika with a fork until foamy.
2. Add the chicken and stir to coat.
3. On a plate, mix the almonds and bread crumbs.
4. Toss the chicken cubes in the almond and bread crumb mixture until coated.
5. Bake the nuggets in the air fryer, in two batches, for 10 to 13 minutes, or until the chicken reaches an internal temperature of 165°F on a meat thermometer. Serve immediately.

Nutrition Info:

• Calories: 249 Fat: 8g (29% of calories from fat) Saturated Fat: 1g Protein: 32g Carbohydrates: 13g Sodium: 137mg Fiber: 3g Sugar: 3g 3% DV vitamin A 2% DV vitamin C

Pork Belly

Servings: 4 | Cooking Time: 40 Minutes

Ingredients:

• 1-pound pork belly, pastured
• 6 cloves of garlic, peeled
• 1 teaspoon ground black pepper
• 1 teaspoon salt
• 2 tablespoons soy sauce
• 2 bay leaves
• 3 cups of water

Directions:

1. Cut the pork belly evenly into three pieces, place them

in an instant pot, and add remaining ingredients.

2. Switch on the instant pot, then shut it with lid and cook the pork belly for 15 minutes at high pressure.

3. When done, let the pressure release naturally for 10 minutes and then do quick pressure release.

4. Rake out the pork by tongs and let it drain and dry for 10 minutes.

5. Then switch on the air fryer, insert fryer basket, grease it with olive oil, then shut with its lid, set the fryer at 400 degrees F and preheat for 5 minutes.

6. While the air fryer preheats, cut each piece of the pork into two long slices.

7. Open the fryer, add pork slices in it, close with its lid and cook for 15 minutes until nicely golden and crispy, flipping the pork halfway through the frying.

8. When air fryer beeps, open its lid, transfer pork slices onto a serving plate and serve.

Nutrition Info:

- Calories: 594 CalCarbs: 2 gFat: 60 gProtein: 11 gFiber: 0 g

Tuna And Fruit Kebabs

Servings: 4 | Cooking Time: 8 To 12 Minutes

Ingredients:

- 1 pound tuna steaks, cut into 1-inch cubes
- ½ cup canned pineapple chunks, drained, juice reserved
- ½ cup large red grapes
- 1 tablespoon honey
- 2 teaspoons grated fresh ginger
- 1 teaspoon olive oil
- Pinch cayenne pepper

Directions:

1. Thread the tuna, pineapple, and grapes on 8 bamboo (see Tip) or 4 metal skewers that fit in the air fryer.

2. In a small bowl, whisk the honey, 1 tablespoon of reserved pineapple juice, the ginger, olive oil, and cayenne. Brush this mixture over the kebabs. Let them stand for 10 minutes.

3. Grill the kebabs for 8 to 12 minutes, or until the tuna reaches an internal temperature of at least 145°F on a meat thermometer, and the fruit is tender and glazed, brushing once with the remaining sauce. Discard any remaining marinade. Serve immediately.

Nutrition Info:

- Calories: 181 Fat: 2g (10% of calories from fat) Saturated Fat: 0g Protein: 18g Carbohydrates: 13g Sodium: 43mg Fiber: 1g Sugar: 12g 3% DV vitamin A 6% DV vitamin C

Air Fryer Meatloaf

Servings: 8 | Cooking Time:40 Minutes

Ingredients:

- Ground lean beef: 4 cups
- Bread crumbs: 1 cup (soft and fresh)
- Chopped mushrooms: ½ cup
- Cloves of minced garlic
- Shredded carrots: ½ cup
- Beef broth: ¼ cup
- Chopped onions: ½ cup
- Two eggs beaten
- Ketchup: 3 Tbsp.
- Worcestershire sauce: 1 Tbsp.
- Dijon mustard: 1 Tbsp.
- For Glaze
- Honey: ¼ cup
- Ketchup: half cup
- Dijon mustard: 2 tsp

Directions:

1. In a big bowl, add beef broth and breadcrumbs, stir well. And set it aside in a food processor, add garlic, onions, mushrooms, and carrots, and pulse on high until finely chopped

2. In a separate bowl, add soaked breadcrumbs, Dijon mustard, Worcestershire sauce, eggs, lean ground beef, ketchup, and salt. With your hands, combine well and make it into a loaf.

3. Let the air fryer preheat to 390 F.

4. Put Meatloaf in the Air Fryer and let it cook for 45 minutes.

5. In the meantime, add Dijon mustard, ketchup, and brown sugar in a bowl and mix. Glaze this mix over Meatloaf when five minutes are left.

6. Rest the Meatloaf for ten minutes before serving.

Nutrition Info:

- Calories 330 |Proteins 19g |Carbs 16g|Fat 9.9 g |

Asian Swordfish

Servings: 4 | Cooking Time: 6 To 11 Minutes

Ingredients:

- 4 (4-ounce) swordfish steaks
- ½ teaspoon toasted sesame oil (see Tip)
- 1 jalapeño pepper, finely minced
- 2 garlic cloves, grated
- 1 tablespoon grated fresh ginger
- ½ teaspoon Chinese five-spice powder
- ⅛ teaspoon freshly ground black pepper
- 2 tablespoons freshly squeezed lemon juice

Directions:

1. Place the swordfish steaks on a work surface and drizzle with the sesame oil.
2. In a small bowl, mix the jalapeño, garlic, ginger, five-spice powder, pepper, and lemon juice. Rub this mixture into the fish and let it stand for 10 minutes.
3. Roast the swordfish in the air fryer for 6 to 11 minutes, or until the swordfish reaches an internal temperature of at least 140°F on a meat thermometer. Serve immediately.

Nutrition Info:

- Calories: 187 Fat: 6g (29% of calories from fat) Saturated Fat: 1g Protein: 29g Carbohydrates: 2g Sodium: 132mg Fiber: 0g Sugar: 1g 3% DV vitamin A 15% DV vitamin C

Whole-wheat Pumpkin Muffins

Servings: 36 | Cooking Time: 15 Minutes

Ingredients:

- 1 ¾-cup whole-wheat flour
- 1-teaspoon baking powder
- 1-teaspoon baking soda
- 1-teaspoon ground cinnamon
- 1-teaspoon pumpkin pie spice
- ½-teaspoon salt
- 2 large eggs
- 1 cup canned pumpkin puree
- 1/3 cup unsweetened applesauce
- ¼-cup light brown sugar
- 1-teaspoon vanilla extract
- 1/3 cup fat-free milk
- Liquid stevia extract, to taste

Directions:

1. Preheat the oven to 350°F and grease two 24-cup mini muffin pans with cooking spray.
2. Whisk together the flour, baking powder, baking soda, cinnamon, pumpkin pie spice, and salt in a large mixing bowl.
3. In a separate bowl, whisk together the eggs, pumpkin, applesauce, brown sugar, vanilla extract, and milk.
4. Stir the wet ingredients into the dry until well combined.
5. Adjust sweetness to taste with liquid stevia extract, if desired.
6. Spoon the batter into 36 cups and bake for 12 to 15 minutes until cooked through.

Nutrition Info:

- Calories: 240 Fat: 12g Carbohydrates: 29g Protein: 4g Sugar: 100g Cholesterol: 67g

Chapter 6: Fish And Seafood Recipes

Chapter 6: Fish And Seafood Recipes

Lemon Garlic Shrimp In Air Fryer

Servings: 2 | Cooking Time:10 Minutes

Ingredients:
- Olive oil: 1 Tbsp.
- Small shrimp: 4 cups, peeled, tails removed
- One lemon juice and zest
- Parsley: 1/4 cup sliced
- Red pepper flakes (crushed): 1 pinch
- Four cloves of grated garlic
- Sea salt: 1/4 teaspoon

Directions:
1. Let air fryer heat to 400F
2. Mix olive oil, lemon zest, red pepper flakes, shrimp, kosher salt, and garlic in a bowl and coat the shrimp well.
3. Place shrimps in the air fryer basket, coat with oil spray.
4. Cook at 400 F for 8 minutes. Toss the shrimp halfway through
5. Serve with lemon slices and parsley.

Nutrition Info:
- Cal 140| Fat: 18g |Net Carbs: 8g|Protein: 20g

Cajun Shrimp In Air Fryer

Servings: 4 | Cooking Time:20 Minutes

Ingredients:
- Peeled, 24 extra-jumbo shrimp
- Olive oil: 2 tablespoons
- Cajun seasoning: 1 tablespoon
- one zucchini, thick slices (half-moons)
- Cooked Turkey: ¼ cup
- Yellow squash, sliced half-moons
- Kosher salt: 1/4 teaspoon

Directions:
1. In a bowl, mix the shrimp with Cajun seasoning.
2. In another bowl, add zucchini, turkey, salt, squash, and coat with oil.
3. Let the air fryer preheat to 400F
4. Move the shrimp and vegetable mix to the fryer basket and cook for three minutes.
5. Serve hot.

Nutrition Info:
- Calories: 284kcal|Carbohydrates: 8g| Protein: 31|Fat: 14g

Breaded Hake

Servings: 4 | Cooking Time: 12 Minutes

Ingredients:
- 1 egg
- oz. Breadcrumbs
- 2 tablespoons vegetable oil
- 6-oz. hake fillets
- 1 lemon cut into wedges

Directions:
1. In a shallow bowl, whisk the egg.
2. In another bowl, add the breadcrumbs and oil and mix until a crumbly mixture form.
3. Dip fish fillets into the egg and then coat with the breadcrumb's mixture.
4. Press the "power button" of air fry oven and turn the dial to select the "air fry" mode.
5. Press the time button and again turn the dial to set the cooking time to 12 minutes.
6. Now push the temp button and rotate the dial to set the temperature at 350 degrees f.
7. Press the "start/pause" button to start.
8. When the unit beeps to show that it is preheated, open the lid. Arrange the hake fillets in greased "air fry basket" and insert in the oven.
9. Serve hot.

Nutrition Info:
- Calories: 297 kcal; Fat: 10.6g; Carbs: 22g; Protein 29.2g

Parmesan Garlic Crusted Salmon

Servings: 2 | Cooking Time:15 Minutes

Ingredients:
- Whole wheat breadcrumbs: 1/4 cup
- 4 cups of salmon
- Butter melted: 2 tablespoons
- ¼ tsp of freshly ground black pepper
- Parmesan cheese: 1/4 cup(grated)
- Minced garlic: 2 teaspoons
- Half teaspoon of Italian seasoning

Directions:
1. Let the air fryer preheat to 400 F, spray the oil over the air fryer basket.
2. Pat dry the salmon. In a bowl, mix Parmesan cheese, Italian seasoning, and breadcrumbs. In another pan, mix melted butter with garlic and add to the breadcrumbs mix. Mix well
3. Add kosher salt and freshly ground black pepper to salmon. On top of every salmon piece, add the crust mix and press gently.

4. Let the air fryer preheat to 400 F and add salmon to it. Cook until done to your liking.
5. Serve hot with vegetable side dishes.

Nutrition Info:

- Calories 330 |Fat 19g|Carbohydrates 11g|Protein 31g

Air Fryer Fish & Chips

Servings: 4 | Cooking Time:35 Minutes

Ingredients:

- 4 cups of any fish fillet
- flour: 1/4 cup
- Whole wheat breadcrumbs: one cup
- One egg
- Oil: 2 tbsp.
- Potatoes
- Salt: 1 tsp.

Directions:

1. Cut the potatoes in fries. Then coat with oil and salt.
2. Cook in the air fryer for 20 minutes at 400 F, toss the fries halfway through.
3. In the meantime, coat fish in flour, then in the whisked egg, and finally in breadcrumbs mix.
4. Place the fish in the air fryer and let it cook at 330F for 15 minutes.
5. Flip it halfway through, if needed.
6. Serve with tartar sauce and salad green.

Nutrition Info:

- Calories: 409kcal | Carbohydrates: 44g | Protein: 30g | Fat: 11g |

Sesame Seeds Coated Tuna

Servings: 2 | Cooking Time: 6 Minutes

Ingredients:

- 1 egg white
- 1/4 cup white sesame seeds
- 1 tbsp. black sesame seeds
- Salt and ground black pepper
- 6-oz. tuna steaks

Directions:

1. In a shallow bowl, beat the egg white.
2. In another bowl, mix the sesame seeds, salt, and black pepper.
3. Dip the tuna steaks into the egg white and then coat with the sesame seeds mixture.
4. Press the "power button" of air fry oven and turn the dial to select the "air fry" mode.
5. Press the time button and again turn the dial to set the cooking time to 6 minutes.
6. Now push the temp button and rotate the dial to set the temperature at 400°F.
7. Press the "start/pause" button to start.
8. When the unit beeps to show that it is preheated, open

the lid.
9. Arrange the tuna steaks in greased "air fry basket" and insert in the oven.
10. Flip the tuna steaks once halfway through.
11. Serve hot.

Nutrition Info:

- Calories: 450 kcal; Fat: 21.9g; Carbs: 5.4g; Protein: 56.7g

Simple Haddock

Servings: 2 | Cooking Time: 8 Minutes

Ingredients:

- 6-oz. haddock fillets
- 1 tbsp. olive oil
- Salt and ground black pepper

Directions:

1. Coat the fish fillets with oil and then sprinkle with salt and black pepper.
2. Press the "power button" of air fry oven and turn the dial to select the "air fry" mode.
3. Press the time button and again turn the dial to set the cooking time to 8 minutes.
4. Now push the temp button and rotate the dial to set the temperature at 355°F.
5. Press the "start/pause" button to start.
6. When the unit beeps to show that it is preheated, open the lid.
7. Arrange the haddock fillets in greased "air fry basket" and insert in the oven.
8. Serve hot.

Nutrition Info:

- Calories: 251 kcal; Fat: 8.6g; Fat: 1.3g; Carbs: 0g; Protein: 41.2g

Baked Salmon

Servings: 2 | Cooking Time: 10 Minutes

Ingredients:

- 2 (6 oz. each) skinless fillets salmon, boneless
- 1 tsp. olive oil.
- Salt
- Black pepper, ground

Directions:

1. Spray equal amounts of oil to the salmon. Season with pepper and salt.
2. Set the fillets in your air fryer basket. Allow to cook for 10 minutes at 360°F. Enjoy.

Nutrition Info:

- Calories: 170g; Fat: 6g; Proteins: 26g; Carbs: 0g

Air Fryer Salmon Fillets

Servings: 2 | Cooking Time:15 Minutes

Ingredients:

- Low-fat Greek yogurt: 1/4 cup
- Two salmon fillets
- Fresh dill: 1 tbsp. (chopped)
- One lemon and lemon juice
- Garlic powder: half tsp.
- Kosher salt and pepper

Directions:

1. Cut the lemon in slices and lay at the bottom of the air fryer basket.
2. Season the salmon with kosher salt and pepper. Put salmon on top of lemons.
3. Let it cook at 330 degrees for 15 minutes.
4. In the meantime, mix garlic powder, lemon juice, salt, pepper with yogurt and dill.
5. Serve the fish with sauce.

Nutrition Info:

- Calories: 194kcal | Carbohydrates: 6g | Protein: 25g | Fat: 7g

Salmon With Brown Sugar Glaze

Servings: 1 | Cooking Time: 15 Minutes

Ingredients:

- 2 tbsps. Dijon mustard
- 4 (6 oz.) Boneless salmon fillets
- 1/4 Cup of packed light brown sugar
- Salt
- Ground black pepper

Directions:

1. Adjust the temperature of the Air Fryer to 3750F.
2. Sprinkle the Fryer basket with cooking spray.
3. Apply pepper and salt on the fish then place it in the Air Fryer basket.
4. In a separate small bowl, whisk together brown sugar and Dijon mustard.
5. Coat the fish properly with the mixture.
6. Cook for about 15 minutes.
7. Serve

Nutrition Info:

- Calories: 553 kcal; Fat: 9.2g; Carbs: 18.3g; Protein: 28.9g

Grilled Salmon With Lemon

Servings: 4 | Cooking Time:20 Minutes

Ingredients:

- Olive oil: 2 tablespoons
- Two Salmon fillets
- Lemon juice
- Water: 1/3 cup
- Gluten-free light soy sauce: 1/3 cup
- Honey: 1/3 cup
- Scallion slices
- Cherry tomato
- Freshly ground black pepper, garlic powder, kosher salt to taste

Directions:

1. Season salmon with pepper and salt
2. In a bowl, mix honey, soy sauce, lemon juice, water, oil. Add salmon in this marinade and let it rest for least two hours.
3. Let the air fryer preheat at 180°C
4. Place fish in the air fryer and cook for 8 minutes.
5. Move to a dish and top with scallion slices.

Nutrition Info:

- Cal 211| fat 9g |protein 15g| carbs 4.9g

Honey-glazed Salmon

Servings: 2 | Cooking Time:15 Minutes

Ingredients:

- Gluten-free Soy Sauce: 6 tsp
- Salmon Fillets: 2 pcs
- Sweet rice wine: 3 tsp
- Water: 1 tsp
- Honey: 6 tbsp.

Directions:

1. In a bowl, mix sweet rice wine, soy sauce, honey, and water.
2. Set half of it aside.
3. In the half of it, marinate the fish and let it rest for two hours.
4. Let the air fryer preheat to 180 C
5. Cook the fish for 8 minutes, flip halfway through and cook for another five minutes.
6. Baste the salmon with marinade mixture after 3 or 4 minutes.
7. The half of marinade, pour in a saucepan reduce to half, serve with a sauce.

Nutrition Info:

- calories 254| carbs 9.9 g| fat 12 g| protein 20 g|

Air Fried Cajun Salmon

Servings: 1 | Cooking Time:20 Minutes

Ingredients:

- Fresh salmon: 1 piece
- Cajun seasoning: 2 tbsp.
- Lemon juice.

Directions:

1. Let the air fryer preheat to 180 C.
2. Pat dry the salmon fillet. Rub lemon juice and Cajun seasoning over the fish fillet.
3. Place in the air fryer, cook for 7 minutes. Serve with salad greens and lime wedges.

Nutrition Info:

- 216 Cal| total fat 19g |carbohydrates 5.6g |protein 19.2g

Catfish With Green Beans, In Southern Style

Servings: 2 | Cooking Time:20 Minutes

Ingredients:

- Catfish fillets: 2 pieces
- Green beans: half cup, trimmed
- Honey: 2 teaspoon
- Freshly ground black pepper and salt, to taste divided
- Crushed red pepper: half tsp.
- Flour: 1/4 cup
- One egg, lightly beaten
- Dill pickle relish: 3/4 teaspoon
- Apple cider vinegar: half tsp
- 1/3 cup whole-wheat breadcrumbs
- Mayonnaise: 2 tablespoons
- Dill
- Lemon wedges

Directions:

1. In a bowl, add green beans, spray them with cooking oil. Coat with crushed red pepper, 1/8 teaspoon of kosher salt, and half tsp. Of honey and cook in the air fryer at 400 F until soft and browned, for 12 minutes. Take out from fryer and cover with aluminum foil
2. In the meantime, coat catfish in flour. Then dip in egg to coat, then in breadcrumbs. Place fish in an air fryer basket and spray with cooking oil.
3. Cook for 8 minutes, at 400°F, until cooked through and golden brown.
4. Sprinkle with pepper and salt. In the meantime, mix vinegar, dill, relish, mayonnaise, and honey in a bowl. Serve the sauce with fish and green beans.

Nutrition Info:

- Cal 243| fat 18 g| Carbs 18 g| Protein 33 g

Crispy Fish Sandwiches

Servings: 2 | Cooking Time:10 Minutes

Ingredients:

- Cod:2 fillets.
- All-purpose flour: 2 tablespoons
- Pepper: 1/4 teaspoon
- Lemon juice: 1 tablespoon
- Salt: 1/4 teaspoon
- Garlic powder: half teaspoon
- One egg
- Mayo: half tablespoon
- Whole wheat bread crumbs: half cup

Directions:

1. In a bowl, add salt, flour, pepper, and garlic powder.
2. In a separate bowl, add lemon juice, mayo, and egg.
3. In another bowl, add the breadcrumbs.
4. Coat the fish in flour, then in egg, then in breadcrumbs.
5. With cooking oil, spray the basket and put the fish in the basket. Also, spray the fish with cooking oil.
6. Cook at 400 F for ten minutes. This fish is soft, be careful if you flip.

Nutrition Info:

- Cal 218| Net Carbs:7g| Fat:12g| Protein: 22g

Air Fryer Tuna Patties

Servings: 10 | Cooking Time:10 Minutes

Ingredients:

- Whole wheat breadcrumbs: half cup
- Fresh tuna: 4 cups, diced
- Lemon zest
- Lemon juice: 1 Tablespoon
- 1 egg
- Grated parmesan cheese: 3 Tablespoons
- One chopped stalk celery
- Garlic powder: half teaspoon
- Dried herbs: half teaspoon
- Minced onion: 3 Tablespoons
- Salt to taste
- Freshly ground black pepper

Directions:

1. In a bowl, add lemon zest, bread crumbs, salt, pepper, celery, eggs, dried herbs, lemon juice, garlic powder, parmesan cheese, and onion. Mix everything. Then add in tuna gently. Shape into patties. If the mixture is too loose, cool in the refrigerator.
2. Add air fryer baking paper in the air fryer basket. Spray the baking paper with cooking spray.
3. Spray the patties with oil.
4. Cook for ten minutes at 360°F. turn the patties halfway over.
5. Serve with lemon slices.

Nutrition Info:

- Cal 214| Fat: 15g| Net Carbs: 6g| Protein: 22g

Sesame Seeds Fish Fillet

Servings: 2 | Cooking Time:20 Minutes

Ingredients:

- Plain flour: 3 tablespoons
- One egg, beaten
- Five frozen fish fillets
- For Coating
- Oil: 2 tablespoons
- Sesame seeds: 1/2 cup
- Rosemary herbs
- 5-6 biscuit's crumbs
- Kosher salt& pepper, to taste

Directions:

1. For two-minute sauté the sesame seeds in a pan, without oil. Brown them and set it aside.
2. In a plate, mix all coating ingredients
3. Place the aluminum foil on the air fryer basket and let it preheat at 200 C.
4. First, coat the fish in flour. Then in egg, then in the coating mix.
5. Place in the Air fryer. If fillets are frozen, cook for ten minutes, then turn the fillet and cook for another four minutes.
6. If not frozen, then cook for eight minutes and two minutes.

Nutrition Info:

- Cal 250| Fat: 8g| Net Carbs: 12.4g| Protein: 20g

Crispy Air Fryer Fish

Servings: 4 | Cooking Time:17 Minutes

Ingredients:

- Old bay: 2 tsp
- 4-6, cut in half, Whiting Fish fillets
- Fine cornmeal: ¾ cup
- Flour: ¼ cup
- Paprika: 1 tsp
- Garlic powder: half tsp
- Salt: 1 and ½ tsp
- Freshly ground black pepper: half tsp

Directions:

1. In a ziploc bag, add all ingredients and coat the fish fillets with it.
2. Spray oil on the basket of air fryer and put the fish in it.
3. Cook for ten minutes at 400 F. flip fish if necessary and coat with oil spray and cook for another seven-minute.
4. Serve with salad green.

Nutrition Info:

- 254 Kcal| fat 12.7g|carbohydrates8.2g |protein 17.5g.

Crispy Fish Sticks In Air Fryer

Servings:4 | Cooking Time:15 Minutes

Ingredients:

- Whitefish such as cod 1 lb.
- Mayonnaise ¼ c
- Dijon mustard 2 tbsp.
- Water 2 tbsp.
- Pork rind 1&1/2 c
- Cajun seasoning ¾ tsp
- Kosher salt& pepper to taste

Directions:

1. Spray non-stick cooking spray to the air fryer rack.
2. Pat the fish dry & cut into sticks about 1 inch by 2 inches' broad
3. Stir together the mayo, mustard, and water in a tiny small dish. Mix the pork rinds & Cajun seasoning into another small container.
4. Adding kosher salt& pepper to taste (both pork rinds & seasoning can have a decent amount of kosher salt, so you can dip a finger to see how salty it is).
5. Working for one slice of fish at a time, dip to cover in the mayo mix & then tap off the excess. Dip into the mixture of pork rind, then flip to cover. Place on the rack of an air fryer.
6. Set at 400F to Air Fry & bake for 5 minutes, then turn the fish with tongs and bake for another 5 minutes. Serve.

Nutrition Info:

- Cal: 263| Fat: 16g| Net Carbs: 1g| Protein: 26.4g

Salmon Cakes In Air Fryer

Servings:2 | Cooking Time:10 Minutes

Ingredients:

- Fresh salmon fillet 8 oz.
- Egg 1
- Salt 1/8 tsp
- Garlic powder ¼ tsp
- Sliced lemon 1

Directions:

1. In the bowl, chop the salmon, add the egg & spices.
2. Form tiny cakes.
3. Let the Air fryer preheat to 390. On the bottom of the air fryer bowl lay sliced lemons—place cakes on top.
4. Cook them for seven minutes. Based on your diet preferences, eat with your chosen dip.

Nutrition Info:

- Kcal: 194, Fat: 9g, Carbs: 1g, Protein: 25g

Shrimp Scampi

Servings: 4 | Cooking Time: 12 Minutes

Ingredients:
- 1-pound shrimp, peeled, deveined
- 1 tablespoon minced garlic
- 1 tablespoon minced basil
- 1 tablespoon lemon juice
- 1 teaspoon dried chives
- 1 teaspoon dried basil
- 2 teaspoons red pepper flakes
- 4 tablespoons butter, unsalted
- 2 tablespoons chicken stock

Directions:
1. Switch on the air fryer, insert fryer pan, grease it with olive oil, then shut with its lid, set the fryer at 330 degrees F and preheat for 5 minutes.
2. Add butter in it along with red pepper and garlic and cook for 2 minutes or until the butter has melted.
3. Then add remaining ingredients in the pan, stir until mixed and continue cooking for 5 minutes until shrimps have cooked, stirring halfway through.
4. When done, remove the pan from the air fryer, stir the shrimp scampi, let it rest for 1 minute and then stir again.
5. Garnish shrimps with basil leaves and serve.

Nutrition Info:
- Calories: 221 CalCarbs: 1 gFat: 13 gProtein: 23 gFiber: 0 g

Salmon

Servings: 2 | Cooking Time: 12 Minutes

Ingredients:
- 2 salmon fillets, wild-caught, each about 1 ½ inch thick
- 1 teaspoon ground black pepper
- 2 teaspoons paprika
- 1 teaspoon salt
- 2 teaspoons olive oil

Directions:
1. Switch on the air fryer, insert fryer basket, grease it with olive oil, then shut with its lid, set the fryer at 390 degrees F and preheat for 5 minutes.
2. Meanwhile, rub each salmon fillet with oil and then season with black pepper, paprika, and salt.
3. Open the fryer, add seasoned salmon in it, close with its lid and cook for 7 minutes until nicely golden and cooked, flipping the fillets halfway through the frying.
4. When air fryer beeps, open its lid, transfer salmon onto a serving plate and serve.

Nutrition Info:
- Calories: 288 CalCarbs: 1.4 gFat: 18.9 gProtein: 28.3 gFiber: 0.8 g

Basil-parmesan Crusted Salmon

Servings: 4 | Cooking Time:15 Minutes

Ingredients:
- Grated Parmesan: 3 tablespoons
- Skinless four salmon fillets
- Salt: 1/4 teaspoon
- Freshly ground black pepper
- Low-fat mayonnaise: 3 tablespoons
- Basil leaves, chopped
- Half lemon

Directions:
1. Let the air fryer preheat to 400F. Spray the basket with olive oil.
2. With salt, pepper, and lemon juice, season the salmon.
3. In a bowl, mix two tablespoons of Parmesan cheese with mayonnaise and basil leaves.
4. Add this mix and more parmesan on top of salmon and cook for seven minutes or until fully cooked.
5. Serve hot.

Nutrition Info:
- Calories: 289kcal|Carbohydrates: 1.5g|Protein: 30g|Fat: 18.5g

Air-fried Fish Nuggets

Servings: 4 | Cooking Time:10 Minutes

Ingredients:
- Fish fillets in cubes: 2 cups(skinless)
- 1 egg, beaten
- Flour: 5 tablespoons
- Water: 5 tablespoons
- Kosher salt and pepper to taste
- Breadcrumbs mix
- Smoked paprika: 1 tablespoon
- Whole wheat breadcrumbs: ¼ cup
- Garlic powder: 1 tablespoon

Directions:
1. Season the fish cubes with kosher salt and pepper.
2. In a bowl, add flour and gradually add water, mixing as you add.
3. Then mix in the egg. And keep mixing but do not over mix.
4. Coat the cubes in batter, then in the breadcrumb mix. Coat well
5. Place the cubes in a baking tray and spray with oil.
6. Let the air fryer preheat to 200 C.
7. Place cubes in the air fryer and cook for 12 minutes or until well cooked and golden brown.
8. Serve with salad greens.

Nutrition Info:
- Cal |184.2|Protein: 19g| Total Fat: 3.3 g| Net Carb: 10g

Crab Cake

Servings: 2 | Cooking Time: 15 Minutes

Ingredients:

- 8 ounces crab meat, wild-caught
- 2 tablespoons almond flour
- 1/4 cup red bell pepper, cored, chopped
- 2 green onion, chopped
- 1 teaspoon old bay seasoning
- 1 tablespoon Dijon mustard
- 2 tablespoons mayonnaise, reduced-fat

Directions:

1. Switch on the air fryer, insert fryer basket, grease it with olive oil, then shut with its lid, set the fryer at 370 degrees F and preheat for 5 minutes.
2. Meanwhile, place all the ingredients in a bowl, stir until well combined and then shape the mixture into four patties.
3. Open the fryer, add crab patties in it, spray oil over the patties, close with its lid and cook for 10 minutes until nicely golden and crispy, flipping the patties halfway through the frying.
4. When air fryer beeps, open its lid, transfer the crab patties onto a serving plate and serve with lemon wedges.

Nutrition Info:

- Calories: 123 CalCarbs: 5 gFat: 6 gProtein: 12 gFiber: 1 g

Mushrooms Stuffed With Tuna

Servings: 4 | Cooking Time: 10 Minutes

Ingredients:

- 8 large mushrooms
- 1 can of tuna
- Mayonnaise

Directions:

1. Remove the trunks to the mushrooms and reserve for another recipe.
2. Peel the mushrooms and place in the basket of the air fryer, face down.
3. Cook for 10 minutes at 1600C.
4. Take out and let cool.
5. In a bowl, mix the well-drained tuna with a little mayonnaise, just to make the tuna juicy and compact.
6. Fill the mushrooms with the tuna and mayonnaise mixture.

Nutrition Info:

- Calories: 150 kcal; Fat: 6g; Carbs: 1g; Protein: 8g

Air Fryer Sushi Roll

Servings: 3 | Cooking Time:10 Minutes

Ingredients:

- For the Kale Salad
- Rice vinegar: half teaspoon
- Chopped kale: one and a 1/2 cups
- Garlic powder:1/8 teaspoon
- Sesame seeds: 1 tablespoon
- Toasted sesame oil: 3/4 teaspoon
- Ground ginger: 1/4 teaspoon
- Soy sauce: 3/4 teaspoon
- Sushi Rolls
- Half avocado - sliced
- Cooked Sushi Rice - cooled
- Whole wheat breadcrumbs: half cup
- Sushi: 3 sheets

Directions:

1. Kale Salad
2. In a bowl, add vinegar, garlic powder, kale, soy sauce, sesame oil, and ground ginger. With your hands, mix with sesame seeds and set it aside.
3. Sushi Rolls
4. Lay a sheet of sushi on a flat surface. With damp fingertips, add a tablespoon of rice, and spread it on the sheet. Cover the sheet with rice, leaving a half-inch space at one end.
5. Add kale salad with avocado slices. Roll up the sushi, use water if needed.
6. Add the breadcrumbs in a bowl. Coat the sushi roll with Sriracha Mayo, then in breadcrumbs.
7. Add the rolls to the air fryer. Cook for ten minutes at 390 F, shake the basket halfway through.
8. Take out from the fryer, and let them cool, then cut with a sharp knife.
9. Serve with light soy sauce.

Nutrition Info:

- Calories: 369cal| Fat: 13.9g|Carbohydrates: 15g|Protein: 26.3g

Air Fried Shrimp With Delicious Sauce

Servings: 4 | Cooking Time:20 Minutes

Ingredients:

- Whole wheat bread crumbs: 3/4 cup
- Raw shrimp: 4 cups, deveined, peeled
- Flour: half cup
- Paprika: one tsp
- Chicken Seasoning, to taste
- 2 tbsp. of one egg white
- Kosher salt and pepper to taste
- Sauce
- Sweet chili sauce: 1/4 cup
- Plain Greek yogurt: 1/3 cup

- Sriracha: 2 tbsp.

Directions:

1. Let the Air Fryer preheat to 400 degrees.
2. Add the seasonings to shrimp and coat well.
3. In three separate bowls, add flour, bread crumbs, and egg whites.
4. First coat the shrimp in flour, dab lightly in egg whites, then in the bread crumbs.
5. With cooking oil, spray the shrimp.
6. Place the shrimps in an air fryer, cook for four minutes, turn the shrimp over, and cook for another four minutes. Serve with micro green and sauce.
7. Sauce
8. In a small bowl, mix all the ingredients. And serve.

Nutrition Info:

- 229 calories| total fat 10g | carbohydrates 13g |protein 22g.

Lemon Pepper Shrimp In Air Fryer

Servings: 2 | Cooking Time:10 Minutes

Ingredients:

- Raw shrimp: 1 and 1/2 cup peeled, deveined
- Olive oil: 1/2 tablespoon
- Garlic powder: ¼ tsp
- Lemon pepper: 1 tsp
- Paprika: ¼ tsp
- Juice of one lemon

Directions:

1. Let the air fryer preheat to 400 F
2. In a bowl, mix lemon pepper, olive oil, paprika, garlic powder, and lemon juice. Mix well. Add shrimps and coat well
3. Add shrimps in the air fryer, cook for 6,8 minutes and top with lemon slices and serve

Nutrition Info:

- Calories 237 |Fat 6g|Carbohydrates 11g|Protein 36g

Fish Finger Sandwich

Servings: 3 | Cooking Time:20 Minutes

Ingredients:

- Greek yogurt: 1 tbsp.
- Cod fillets: 4, without skin
- Flour: 2 tbsp.
- Whole-wheat breadcrumbs: 5 tbsp.
- Kosher salt and pepper to taste
- Capers: 10–12
- Frozen peas: 3/4 cup
- Lemon juice

Directions:

1. Let the air fryer preheat.
2. Sprinkle kosher salt and pepper on the cod fillets, and coat in flour, then in breadcrumbs
3. Spray the fryer basket with oil. Put the cod fillets in the basket.
4. Cook for 15 minutes at 200 C.
5. In the meantime, cook the peas in boiling water for a few minutes. Take out from the water and blend with Greek yogurt, lemon juice, and capers until well combined.
6. On a bun, add cooked fish with pea puree. Add lettuce and tomato.

Nutrition Info:

- Cal 240| Fat: 12g| Net Carbs: 7g| Protein: 20g

Scallops With Creamy Tomato Sauce

Servings: 2 | Cooking Time:10 Minutes

Ingredients:

- Sea scallops eight jumbo
- Tomato Paste: 1 tbsp.
- Chopped fresh basil one tablespoon
- 3/4 cup of low-fat Whipping Cream
- Kosher salt half teaspoon
- Ground Freshly black pepper half teaspoon
- Minced garlic 1 teaspoon
- Frozen Spinach, thawed half cup
- Oil Spray

Directions:

1. Take a seven-inch pan (heatproof) and add spinach in a single layer at the bottom
2. Rub olive oil on both sides of scallops, season with kosher salt and pepper.
3. on top of the spinach, place the seasoned scallops
4. Put the pan in the air fryer and cook for ten minutes at 350F, until scallops are cooked completely, and internal temperature reaches 135F.
5. Serve immediately.

Nutrition Info:

- Calories: 259kcal | Carbohydrates: 6g | Protein: 19g | Fat: 13g |

Coconut Shrimp

Servings:4 | Cooking Time:30 Minutes

Ingredients:

- Pork Rinds: ½ cup (Crushed)
- Jumbo Shrimp:4 cups. (deveined)
- Coconut Flakes preferably: ½ cup
- Eggs: two
- Flour of coconut: ½ cup
- Any oil of your choice for frying at least half-inch in pan
- Freshly ground black pepper & kosher salt to taste
- Dipping sauce (Pina colada flavor)
- Powdered Sugar as Substitute: 2-3 tablespoon
- Mayonnaise: 3 tablespoons
- Sour Cream: ½ cup
- Coconut Extract or to taste: ¼ tsp

- Coconut Cream: 3 tablespoons
- Pineapple Flavoring as much to taste: ¼ tsp
- Coconut Flakes preferably unsweetened this is optional: 3 tablespoons

Directions:

1. Pina Colada (Sauce)
2. Mix all the ingredients into a tiny bowl for the Dipping sauce (Pina colada flavor). Combine well and put in the fridge until ready to serve.
3. Shrimps
4. Whip all eggs in a deep bowl, and a small, shallow bowl, add the crushed pork rinds, coconut flour, sea salt, coconut flakes, and freshly ground black pepper.
5. Put the shrimp one by one in the mixed eggs for dipping, then in the coconut flour blend. Put them on a clean plate or put them on your air fryer's basket.
6. Place the shrimp battered in a single layer on your air fryer basket. Spritz the shrimp with oil and cook for 8-10 minutes at 360 ° F, flipping them through halfway.
7. Enjoy hot with dipping sauce.

Nutrition Info:

- Calories 340 |Proteins 25g |Carbs 9g |Fat 16g |Fiber 7g

Garlic Rosemary Grilled Prawns

Servings: 2 | Cooking Time:10 Minutes

Ingredients:

- Melted butter: 1/2 tbsp.
- Green capsicum: slices
- Eight prawns
- Rosemary leaves
- Kosher salt& freshly ground black pepper
- 3-4 cloves of minced garlic

Directions:

1. In a bowl, mix all the ingredients and marinate the prawns in it for at least 60 minutes or more
2. Add two prawns and two slices of capsicum on each skewer.
3. Let the air fryer preheat to 180 C.
4. Cook for 5-6 minutes. Then change the temperature to 200 C and cook for another minute.
5. Serve with lemon wedges.

Nutrition Info:

- Cal 194 |Fat: 10g|Carbohydrates: 12g|protein: 26g

Breaded Hake With Green Chili Pepper And Mayonnaise

Servings: 4 | Cooking Time: 20 Minutes

Ingredients:

- 4 breaded hake fillets
- Mayonnaise
- Green mojito
- Extra virgin olive oil

Directions:

1. Paint the breaded hake fillets with extra virgin olive oil.
2. Put them in the air fryer basket and cook at 1800C for 30 minutes.
3. Meanwhile, put in a bowl 8 teaspoons of mayonnaise and 2 of green mojito.
4. Let flirt well.
5. Serve the breaded hake fillets with the green mojito mayonnaise.

Nutrition Info:

- Calories: 132 kcal; Fat: 4.38g; Carbs: 0.41g; Protein: 21.38g

Fish Sticks

Servings: 4 | Cooking Time: 15 Minutes

Ingredients:

- 1-pound cod, wild-caught
- ½ teaspoon ground black pepper
- 3/4 teaspoon Cajun seasoning
- 1 teaspoon salt
- 1 1/2 cups pork rind
- 1/4 cup mayonnaise, reduced-fat
- 2 tablespoons water
- 2 tablespoons Dijon mustard

Directions:

1. Switch on the air fryer, insert fryer basket, grease it with olive oil, then shut with its lid, set the fryer at 400 degrees F and preheat for 5 minutes.
2. Meanwhile, place mayonnaise in a bowl and then whisk in water and mustard until blended.
3. Place pork rinds in a shallow dish, add Cajun seasoning, black pepper and salt and stir until mixed.
4. Cut the cod into 1 by 2 inches pieces, then dip into mayonnaise mixture and then coat with pork rind mixture.
5. Open the fryer, add fish sticks in it, spray with oil, close with its lid and cook for 10 minutes until nicely golden and crispy, flipping the sticks halfway through the frying.
6. When air fryer beeps, open its lid, transfer fish sticks onto a serving plate and serve.

Nutrition Info:

- Calories: 263 CalCarbs: 1 gFat: 16 gProtein: 26.4 gFiber: 0.5 g

Air Fryer Crab Cakes

Servings: 6 | Cooking Time:20 Minutes

Ingredients:

- Crab meat: 4 cups
- Two eggs
- Whole wheat bread crumbs: ¼ cup
- Mayonnaise: 2 tablespoons
- Worcestershire sauce: 1 teaspoon
- Old Bay seasoning: 1 and ½ teaspoon
- Dijon mustard: 1 teaspoon
- Freshly ground black pepper to taste
- Green onion: ¼ cup, chopped

Directions:

1. In a bowl, add Dijon mustard, Old Bay, eggs, Worcestershire, and mayonnaise mix it well. Then add in the chopped green onion and mix.
2. Fold in the crab meat to mayonnaise mix. Then add breadcrumbs, not to over mix.
3. Chill the mix in the refrigerator for at least 60 minutes. Then shape into patties.
4. Let the air-fryer preheat to 350F. Cook for 10 minutes. Flip the patties halfway through.
5. Serve with lemon wedges.

Nutrition Info:

- Cal 218| Fat: 13 g| Net Carbs: 5.6 g| Protein: 16.7g

Air Fryer Salmon With Maple Soy Glaze

Servings: 4 | Cooking Time:8 Minutes

Ingredients:

- Pure maple syrup: 3 tbsp.
- Gluten-free soy sauce: 3 tbsp.
- Sriracha hot sauce: 1 tbsp.
- One clove of minced garlic
- Salmon: 4 fillets, skinless

Directions:

1. In a ziploc bag, mix sriracha, maple syrup, garlic, and soy sauce with salmon.
2. Mix well and let it marinate for at least half an hour.
3. Let the air fryer preheat to 400F with oil spray the basket
4. Take fish out from the marinade, pat dry.
5. Put the salmon in the air fryer, cook for 7 to 8 minutes, or longer.
6. In the meantime, in a saucepan, add the marinade, let it simmer until reduced to half.
7. Add glaze over salmon and serve.

Nutrition Info:

- Calories 292| Carbohydrates: 12g| Protein: 35g|Fat: 11g|

Shrimp Spring Rolls In Air Fryer

Servings: 4 | Cooking Time:25 Minutes

Ingredients:

- Deveined raw shrimp: half cup chopped (peeled)
- Olive oil: 2 and 1/2 tbsp.
- Matchstick carrots: 1 cup
- Slices of red bell pepper: 1 cup
- Red pepper: 1/4 teaspoon (crushed)
- Slices of snow peas: 3/4 cup
- Shredded cabbage: 2 cups
- Lime juice: 1 tablespoon
- Sweet chili sauce: half cup
- Fish sauce: 2 teaspoons
- Eight spring roll (wrappers)

Directions:

1. In a skillet, add one and a half tbsp. of olive, until smoking lightly. Stir in bell pepper, cabbage, carrots, and cook for two minutes. Turn off the heat, take out in a dish and cool for five minutes.
2. In a bowl, add shrimp, lime juice, cabbage mixture, crushed red pepper, fish sauce, and snow peas. Mix well
3. Lay spring roll wrappers on a plate. Add 1/4 cup of filling in the middle of each wrapper. Fold tightly with water. Brush the olive oil over folded rolls.
4. Put spring rolls in the air fryer basket and cook for 6 to 7 minutes at 390°F until light brown and crispy.
5. You may serve with sweet chili sauce.

Nutrition Info:

- Calories 180 |Fat 9g| Protein 17g |Carbohydrate 9g

Air Fryer Lemon Cod

Servings: 1 | Cooking Time:10 Minutes

Ingredients:

- One cod fillet
- Dried parsley
- Kosher salt and pepper to taste
- Garlic powder
- One lemon

Directions:

1. In a bowl, mix all ingredients and coat the fish fillet with spices.
2. Slice the lemon and lay at the bottom of the air fryer basket.
3. Put spiced fish on top. Cover the fish with lemon slices.
4. Cook for ten minutes at 375F, the internal temperature of fish should be 145F.
5. Serve with microgreen salad.

Nutrition Info:

- Calories: 101kcal | Carbohydrates: 10g | Protein: 16g | Fat: 1g |

Shrimp With Lemon And Chile

Servings: 2 | Cooking Time: 12 Minutes

Ingredients:

- 1-pound shrimp, wild-caught, peeled, deveined
- 1 lemon, sliced
- 1 small red chili pepper, sliced
- ½ teaspoon ground black pepper
- 1/2 teaspoon garlic powder
- 1 teaspoon salt
- 1 tablespoon olive oil

Directions:

1. Switch on the air fryer, insert fryer basket, grease it with olive oil, then shut with its lid, set the fryer at 400 degrees F and preheat for 5 minutes.
2. Meanwhile, place shrimps in a bowl, add garlic, salt, black pepper, oil, and lemon slices and toss until combined.
3. Open the fryer, add shrimps and lemon in it, close with its lid and cook for 5 minutes, shaking halfway through the frying.
4. Then add chili slices, shake the basket until mixed and continue cooking for 2 minutes or until shrimps are opaque and crispy.
5. When air fryer beeps, open its lid, transfer shrimps and lemon slices onto a serving plate and serve.

Nutrition Info:

- Calories: 112.5 CalCarbs: 1 gFat: 1 gProtein: 20.4 gFiber: 0.2 g

Juicy Air Fryer Salmon

Servings: 4 | Cooking Time:12 Minutes

Ingredients:

- Lemon pepper seasoning: 2 teaspoons
- Salmon: 4 cups
- Olive oil: one tablespoon
- Seafood seasoning:2 teaspoons
- Half lemon's juice
- Garlic powder:1 teaspoon
- Kosher salt to taste

Directions:

1. In a bowl, add one tbsp. of olive oil and half lemon's juice.
2. Pour this mixture over salmon and rub. Leave the skin on salmon. It will come off when cooked.
3. Rub the salmon with kosher salt and spices.
4. Put parchment paper in the air fryer basket. Put the salmon in the air fryer.
5. Cook at 360 F for ten minutes. Cook until inner salmon temperature reaches 140 F.
6. Let the salmon rest five minutes before serving.
7. Serve with salad greens and lemon wedges.

Nutrition Info:

- 132 Cal| total fat 7.4g |carbohydrates 12 g| protein 22.1g

Celery Leaves And Garlic-oil Grilled

Servings: 1 | Cooking Time: 20 Minutes

Ingredients:

- 1/2 mug chopped celery leaves.
- 1 diced clove garlic.
- 2 tbsps. olive oil.
- 2 entire turbot scaled and head got rid of.
- Salt and pepper

Directions:

1. Preheat the air fryer to 390ºF.
2. Arrange the grill frying pan device in the air fryer.
3. Season the turbot with salt, pepper, garlic, as well as celery leaves.
4. Brush with oil.
5. Place on the grill pan and cook for 20 mins up until the fish ends up being flaky.

Nutrition Info:

- Calories: 269 kcal; Carbs: 3.3g; Protein: 66.2g; Fat:25.6g

Salmon Cakes

Servings: 2 | Cooking Time: 12 Minutes

Ingredients:

- ½ cup almond flour
- 15 ounces cooked pink salmon
- ¼ teaspoon ground black pepper
- 2 teaspoons Dijon mustard
- 2 tablespoons chopped fresh dill
- 2 tablespoons mayonnaise, reduced-fat
- 1 egg, pastured
- 2 wedges of lemon

Directions:

1. Switch on the air fryer, insert fryer basket, grease it with olive oil, then shut with its lid, set the fryer at 400 degrees F and preheat for 5 minutes.
2. Meanwhile, place all the ingredients in a bowl, except for lemon wedges, stir until combined and then shape into four patties, each about 4-inches.
3. Open the fryer, add salmon patties in it, spray oil over them, close with its lid and cook for 12 minutes until nicely golden and crispy, flipping the patties halfway through the frying.
4. When air fryer beeps, open its lid, transfer salmon patties onto a serving plate and serve.

Nutrition Info:

- Calories: 517 CalCarbs: 15 gFat: 27 gProtein: 52 gFiber: 5 g

Parmesan Shrimp

Servings: 6 | Cooking Time: 10 Minutes

Ingredients:

- 2 pounds jumbo shrimp, wild-caught, peeled, deveined
- 2 tablespoons minced garlic
- 1 teaspoon onion powder
- 1 teaspoon basil
- 1 teaspoon ground black pepper
- 1/2 teaspoon dried oregano
- 2 tablespoons olive oil
- 2/3 cup grated parmesan cheese, reduced-fat
- 2 tablespoons lemon juice

Directions:

1. Switch on the air fryer, insert fryer basket, grease it with olive oil, then shut with its lid, set the fryer at 350 degrees F and preheat for 5 minutes.
2. Meanwhile, place cheese in a bowl, add remaining ingredients except for shrimps and lemon juice and stir until combined.
3. Add shrimps and then toss until well coated.
4. Open the fryer, add shrimps in it, spray oil over them, close with its lid and cook for 10 minutes until nicely golden and crispy, shaking halfway through the frying.
5. When air fryer beeps, open its lid, transfer chicken onto a serving plate, drizzle with lemon juice and serve.

Nutrition Info:

- Calories: 307 CalCarbs: 12 gFat: 16.4 gProtein: 27.6 gFiber: 3 g

Cajun Experienced Salmon Filet

Servings: 1 | Cooking Time: 15 Minutes

Ingredients:

- 1 salmon fillet.
- 1 tsp. Freshly squeezed juice from lemon.
- 3 tbsps. Extra virgin olive oil.
- A dash Cajun flavoring mix.
- Salt and pepper.

Directions:

1. Preheat the air fryer for 5 minutes.
2. Place all components in a dish and toss to coat.
3. Set the fish fillet in the air fryer basket.
4. Cook for 15 mins at 325°F.
5. Once cooked drizzle with olive oil.

Nutrition Info:

- Calories: 523 kcal; Carbs: 4.6g; Protein: 47.9g; Fat: 34.8g

Tomato Basil Scallops

Servings: 2 | Cooking Time: 15 Minutes

Ingredients:

- 8 jumbo sea scallops, wild-caught
- 1 tablespoon tomato paste
- 12 ounces frozen spinach, thawed and drained
- 1 tablespoon chopped fresh basil
- 1 teaspoon ground black pepper
- 1 teaspoon minced garlic
- 1 teaspoon salt
- 3/4 cup heavy whipping cream, reduced-fat

Directions:

1. Switch on the air fryer, insert fryer basket, grease it with olive oil, then shut with its lid, set the fryer at 350 degrees F and preheat for 5 minutes.
2. Meanwhile, take a 7 inches baking pan, grease it with oil and place spinach in it in an even layer.
3. Spray the scallops with oil, sprinkle with ½ teaspoon each of salt and black pepper and then place scallops over the spinach.
4. Place tomato paste in a bowl, whisk in cream, basil, garlic, and remaining salt and black pepper until smooth, and then pour over the scallops.
5. Open the fryer, place the pan in it, close with its lid and cook for 10 minutes until thoroughly cooked and sauce is hot.
6. Serve straight away.

Nutrition Info:

- Calories: 359 CalCarbs: 6 gFat: 33 gProtein: 9 gFiber: 1 g

Salmon Patties

Servings: 1 | Cooking Time: 5 Minutes

Ingredients:

- 14.75 oz. salmon.
- 1 egg.
- 1/4 mug diced onion.
- 1/2 mug bread crumbs.
- 1 tsp. dill weed.

Directions:

1. Start by cleaning the fish, eliminate the bones and also skin. Drain it.
2. Blend the egg, onion, dill weed, as well as breadcrumbs into the salmon. Mix well.
3. Shape into patties. Position them in the air fryer. Set the temperature level at 370F. For 5 minutes, after that turn them and also air fry for 5 more minutes.
4. Serve.

Nutrition Info:

- Calories: 290 kcal; Carbs: 1.2g; Protein: 27.g; Fat:18.9g

Air Fryer Shrimp Scampi

Servings: 2 | Cooking Time:10 Minutes

Ingredients:

- Raw Shrimp: 4 cups
- Lemon Juice: 1 tablespoon
- Chopped fresh basil
- Red Pepper Flakes: 2 teaspoons
- Butter: 2.5 tablespoons
- Chopped chives
- Chicken Stock: 2 tablespoons
- Minced Garlic: 1 tablespoon

Directions:

1. Let the air fryer preheat with a metal pan to 330F
2. In the hot pan, add garlic, red pepper flakes, and half of the butter. Let it cook for two minutes.
3. Add the butter, shrimp, chicken stock, minced garlic, chives, lemon juice, basil to the pan. Let it cook for five minutes. Bathe the shrimp in melted butter.
4. Take out from the air fryer and let it rest for one minute.
5. Add fresh basil leaves and chives and serve.

Nutrition Info:

- 287 Kcal |total fat 5.5g |carbohydrates 7.5g | protein 18g

Fish With Maille Dijon Originale Mustard

Servings: 1 | Cooking Time: 5 Minutes

Ingredients:

- 4 tsps. Maille Dijon Originale mustard
- 4 thick trimmed cod steaks
- 2 tbsps. Oil
- 1 tbsp. flat parsley

Directions:

1. Adjust the temperature of the Air Fryer to 3500F.
2. Season the trimmed fish.
3. Spray Maille Dijon Originale mustard on the top side of the cod using a pastry brush.
4. Place the fish in the Air Fryer basket.
5. Cook the meal at 4000F for 5 minutes.
6. Once cooked, you can top it with parsley.
7. Serve

Nutrition Info:

- Calories: 383 kcal; Fat: 1.8g; Carbs: 3.6g; Protein: 40.9g

Roasted Salmon With Fennel Salad

Servings: 4 | Cooking Time:10 Minutes

Ingredients:

- Skinless and center-cut: 4 salmon fillets
- Lemon juice: 1 teaspoon (fresh)
- Parsley: 2 teaspoons (chopped)
- Salt: 1 teaspoon, divided
- Olive oil: 2 tablespoons
- Chopped thyme: 1 teaspoon
- Fennel heads: 4 cups (thinly sliced)
- One clove of minced garlic
- Fresh dill: 2 tablespoons, chopped
- Orange juice: 2 tablespoons (fresh)
- Greek yogurt: 2/3 cup (reduced-fat)

Directions:

1. In a bowl, add half teaspoon of salt, parsley, and thyme, mix well. Rub oil over salmon, and sprinkle with thyme mixture.
2. Put salmon fillets in the air fryer basket, cook for ten minutes at 350°F.
3. In the meantime, mix garlic, fennel, orange juice, yogurt, half tsp. of salt, dill, lemon juice in a bowl.
4. Serve with fennel salad.

Nutrition Info:

- Calories 364|Fat 30g|Protein 38g|Carbohydrate 9g

Chapter 7: Other Favorite Recipes

Chapter 7: Other Favorite Recipes

Air Fried Section And Tomato

Servings: 2

Ingredients:

- 1 aubergine, sliced thickly into 4 disks
- 1 tomato, sliced into 2 thick disks
- 2 tsp. feta cheese, reduced fat
- 2 fresh basil leaves, minced
- 2 balls, small buffalo mozzarella, reduced fat, roughly torn
- Pinch of salt
- Pinch of black pepper

Directions:

1. Preheat Air Fryer to 330 degrees F.
2. Spray small amount of oil into the Air fryer basket. Fry aubergine slices for 5 minutes or until golden brown on both sides. Transfer to a plate.
3. Fry tomato slices in batches for 5 minutes or until seared on both sides.
4. To serve, stack salad starting with an aubergine base, buffalo mozzarella, basil leaves, tomato slice, and ½-teaspoon feta cheese.
5. Top of with another slice of aubergine and ½ tsp. feta cheese. Serve.

Nutrition Info:

- Calorie: 140.3Carbohydrate: 26.6Fat: 3.4g Protein: 4.2g Fiber: 7.3g

Chicken Mushroom Stroganoff

Servings: 6 | Cooking Time: 25 Minutes

Ingredients:

- 1 cup fat-free sour cream
- 2 tablespoons flour
- 1 tablespoon Worcestershire sauce
- ½ teaspoon dried thyme
- 1 chicken bouillon cube, crushed
- Salt and pepper
- ½ cup water
- 1 medium yellow onion, chopped
- 8 ounces sliced mushrooms
- 1 tablespoon olive oil
- 2 cloves minced garlic
- 12 ounces boneless skinless chicken breast, cooked and shredded
- 6 ounces whole-wheat noodles, cooked

Directions:

1. Whisk together 2/3 cup of the sour cream with the flour, Worcestershire sauce, thyme, and crushed bouillon in a medium bowl.
2. Season with salt and pepper then slowly stir in the water until well combined.
3. Heat the oil in a large skillet over medium-high heat.
4. Add the onions, mushrooms, and sauté for 3 minutes.
5. Stir in the garlic and cook for 2 minutes more then add the chicken.
6. Pour in the sour cream mixture and cook until thick and bubbling.
7. Reduce heat and simmer for 2 minutes.
8. Spoon the chicken and mushroom mixture over the cooked noodles and garnish with the remaining sour cream to serve.

Nutrition Info:

- Calories 295, Total Fat 7.8g, saturated Fat 2g,Carbs 29.6g,Net Carbs 26.7g, Protein 24.6g, Sugar 4.7g, Fiber 2.9g, Sodium 225mg

Air Fryer Roasted Garlic

Servings: 1 | Cooking Time: 30 Minutes

Ingredients:

- 2 heads garlic.
- 1 tsp olive oil.

Directions:

1. Cut the tops off of the garlic heads, exposing the specific cloves.
2. Arrange the bulbs in the middle of an item of foil and drizzle olive oil over the tops of the garlic bulbs. Pro pointer: the amount of olive oil required will depend on the dimension of garlic heads you are making use of.
3. Tightly finish up the garlic in the aluminum foil and location in the basket of your air fryer.
4. Cook for 27 mins at 400°F.
5. The delicately browns the top of the light bulbs.

Nutrition Info:

- Calories: 31 kcal; Carbs: 5g; Protein: 1g; Fat: 1g

Meatballs In Spicy Tomato Sauce

Servings:4

Ingredients:

- 3 green onions, minced
- 1 garlic clove, minced
- 1 egg yolk
- ¼-cup saltine cracker crumbs
- Pinch salt
- Freshly ground black pepper
- 1 pound 95 percent lean ground beef
- Olive oil for misting
- 1¼ cups pasta sauce

- 2 tablespoons Dijon mustard

Directions:

1. In a large bowl, combine the green onions, garlic, egg yolk, cracker crumbs, salt, and pepper, and mix well.
2. Add the ground beef and mix gently but thoroughly with your hands until combined. Form into 1½-inch meatballs.
3. Mist the meatballs with olive oil and put into the basket of the air fryer
4. Bake for 8 to 11 minutes or until the meatballs are 165°F.
5. Remove the meatballs from the basket and place in a 6-inch metal bowl. Top with the pasta sauce and Dijon mustard and mix gently
6. Bake for 4 minutes until the sauce is hot.

Nutrition Info:

- Calories: 360; Total Fat: 12g; Saturated Fat: 4g; Cholesterol: 154mg; sodium: 875mg; Carbohydrates: 24g; Fiber: 3g; Protein: 39g

Fried Avocado

Servings: 2 | Cooking Time: 10 Minutes

Ingredients:

- 2 avocados cut into wedges 25 mm thick
- 50g Pan crumbs bread
- 2g garlic powder
- 2g onion powder
- 1g smoked paprika
- 1g cayenne pepper
- Salt and pepper to taste
- 60g all-purpose flour
- 2 eggs, beaten
- Nonstick Spray Oil
- Tomato sauce or ranch sauce, to serve

Directions:

1. Cut the avocados into 25 mm thick pieces.
2. Combine the crumbs, garlic powder, onion powder, smoked paprika, cayenne pepper and salt in a bowl.
3. Separate each wedge of avocado in the flour, then dip the beaten eggs and stir in the breadcrumb mixture.
4. Preheat the air fryer.
5. Place the avocados in the preheated air fryer baskets, spray with oil spray and cook at 205°C for 10 minutes. Turn the fried avocado halfway through cooking and sprinkle with cooking oil.
6. Serve with tomato sauce or ranch sauce.

Nutrition Info:

- Calories: 123 Cal Carbs: 2 g Fat: 11 g Protein: 4 g Fiber: 0 g

Air Fryer Party Meatballs

Ingredients:

- 3 crushed gingersnaps
- ½ teaspoon of dry mustard
- ½ cup of brown sugar
- 1 tablespoon of lemon juice
- ¼ cup of vinegar
- 2 ½ tablespoon of Worcester sauce
- 1 tablespoon of Tabasco
- ¾ cup of tomato ketchup
- 1 lb of minced beef

Directions:

1. Add all the seasonings in a large bowl and mix them very well. The mixture has to be even
2. Now, add the minced beef to the bowl and mix them up again.
3. Mold it in several medium-sized meatballs and place them in your air fryer basket.
4. Set your air fryer temperature to 375 degrees F and cook the meatballs for 15 minutes.
5. When they ate done, you can place them on sticks before serving.

Nutrition Info:

- Calories: 483 kcal Carbohydrate: 48g Protein: 20g Fat: 23g Saturated Fat: 9g Cholesterol: 81mg Sodium: 1015mg Potassium: 842mg Fiber: 1g Vitamin A: 265IU Vitamin C: 11.6mg Calcium 98mg Iron: 5mg

Turkey Breast With Mustard Maple Glaze

Servings: 6 | Cooking Time:55 Minutes

Ingredients:

- Whole turkey breast: 5 pounds
- Olive oil: 2 tsp.
- Maple syrup: 1/4 cup
- Dried sage: half tsp.
- Smoked paprika: half tsp.
- Dried thyme: one tsp.
- Salt: one tsp.
- Freshly ground black pepper: half tsp.
- Dijon mustard: 2 tbsp.

Directions:

1. Let the air fryer preheat to 350 F
2. Rub the olive oil all over the turkey breast
3. In a bowl, mix salt, sage, pepper, thyme, and paprika. Mix well and coat turkey in this spice rub.
4. Place the turkey in an air fryer, cook for 25 minutes at 350ºF. Flip the turkey over and cook for another 12 minutes. Flip again and cook for another ten minutes. With an instant-read thermometer, the internal temperature should reach 165ºF.
5. In the meantime, in a saucepan, mix mustard, maple syr-

up, and with one tsp. of butter.

6. Brush this glaze all over the turkey when cooked.

7. Cook again for five minutes. Slice and Serve with fresh salad.

Nutrition Info:

• Cal 379 | Fat: 23 g| Carbs: 21g | Protein: 52g

Creamy Halibut

Servings: 6 | Cooking Time: 20 Minutes

Ingredients:

• 2 lbs. halibut fillets cut into 6 pieces
• 1 tsp. dried dill weed
• 1/2 cup light sour cream
• 1/2 cup light mayonnaise
• 4 chopped green onions

Directions:

1. Adjust the temperature of the air fryer to 390°F.
2. Season the halibut with salt and pepper.
3. Mix the onions, sour cream, mayonnaise, and dill in a bowl.
4. Spread the onion mixture evenly over the halibut fillets. Cook in the air fryer for 20 minutes. Serve warm.

Nutrition Info:

• Calories: 286 kcal; Fat: 11.3g; Carbs: 6.9g; Protein: 29.8g

Air Fryer Sugar-free Lemon Slice & Bake Cookies

Servings: 24 | Cooking Time: 5 Minutes

Ingredients:

• Half teaspoon of salt
• Half cup of coconut flour
• Half cup of unsalted butter softened
• Half teaspoon of liquid vanilla stevia
• Half cup of swerve granular sweetener
• One tablespoon lemon juice
• Lemon extract: 1/4 tsp, it is optional
• Two egg yolks
• For icing
• Three tsp of lemon juice
• 2/3 cup of Swerve confectioner's sweetener

Directions:

1. In a stand mixer bowl, add baking soda, coconut flour, salt and Swerve, mix until well combined
2. Then add the butter (softened) to the dry ingredients, mix well. Add all the remaining ingredients but do not add in the yolks yet. Adjust the seasoning of lemon flavor and sweetness to your liking, add more if needed.
3. Add the yolk and combine well.
4. Lay a big piece of plastic wrap on a flat surface, put the batter in the center, roll around the dough and make it into

a log form, for almost 12 inches. Keep this log in the fridge for 2-3 hours or overnight, if possible.

5. Let the oven preheat to 325 F. generously spray the air fryer basket, take the log out from plastic wrap only unwrap how much you want to use it, and keep the rest in the fridge.

6. Cut in 1/4 inch cookies, place as many cookies in the air fryer basket in one single, do not overcrowd the basket.

7. Bake for 3-five minutes, or until the cookies' edges become brown. Let it cool in the basket for two minutes, then take out from the basket. And let them cool on a wire rack.

8. Once all cookies are baked, pour the icing over. Serve and enjoy.

Nutrition Info:

• Amount Per Serving: Calories 66| Fat 6g|Carbohydrates 2g|Fiber 1g| Sugar 1g|Protein 1g

Mini Turkey Meatballs

Ingredients:

• 3 tablespoons of olive oil
• 3 tablespoons of ketchup
• 3 garlic cloves, minced
• 1/4 teaspoon of ground black pepper
• 1/4 cup of grated Pecorino Romano
• 1/4 cup of grated Parmesan
• 1/4 cup of dried bread crumbs
• 1/4 cup of chopped fresh Italian parsley leaves
• 1 teaspoon of salt
• 1 small onion, grated
• 1 pound of ground dark turkey meat
• 1 large egg

Directions:

1. Get a big bowl. Add pepper, salt, Pecorino, Parmesan, parsley, ketchup, bread crumbs, egg, garlic, and onion together. Whisk them until they mix evenly. Add the turkey and mix them together.
2. Shape the mixture into several meatballs. Air fry the meatballs for about 5 minutes. They should be brown by them.
3. Now prepare your favorite sauce and dredge the meatballs in it.You can now serve the turkey meatballs. They are best served either warm or hot.

Nutrition Info:

• Calories: 48 Total Fat: 3g Cholesterol:15mg Sodium: 180mg Carbohydrates: 3g Protein: 3g

Air Fried Pickle Chips

Ingredients:

- 2 large eggs
- 1 teaspoon of lemon juice
- 1 tablespoon of Creole mustard
- 1 jar of reduced-sodium dill pickle chips
- 1 cup of panko breadcrumbs
- ½ teaspoon of smoked paprika
- ½ cup of all-purpose flour
- ¼ cup of mayonnaise

Directions:

1. Beat the eggs in a small bowl lightly.
2. Pour the flour into another bowl and place the panko in a third bowl.
3. Drain the pickle chips before patting them dry with paper towels.
4. Now, soak the pickle chips in the flour and shake off excess. Just ensure that they are well coated.
5. After dipping the in flour, you need to dip them in the beaten eggs. Now, you can toss the coated pickles in panko.
6. Divide the pickles into three batches so that you can air fry them batch by batch.
7. Cook the first batch at 350 degrees F for 6 minutes. They should be tender, crispy, and golden brown by then.
8. Do the same to the remaining two batches.
9. Mix the smoked paprika, lemon juice, Creole mustard, and mayonnaise together in another bowl. Serve the pickle chips with the mayonnaise mixture as dipping sauce.

Nutrition Info:

- Calories: 177 Total Fat: 9.1g Saturated Fat: 1.6g Cholesterol: 66mg Sodium: 409mg Potassium: 86mg Carbohydrates: 18.6g Fiber: 2.1g Protein: 5.6g Vitamin C: 1mg Calcium: 34mg Iron: 1mg Magnesium: 8mg

Crispy Hen Tenders

Servings: 6 | Cooking Time: 20 Minutes

Ingredients:

- 20 halved Chicken Tenders
- 1 mug mayo
- 2 cups panko
- Salt

Directions:

1. Arrange panko in a medium-size dish. Set aside.
2. Location reduced chicken in a big bowl with mayonnaise - throw to layer.
3. Dealing with 1-2 items each time, transfer layered chicken to panko bowl & toss to layer.
4. Arrange panko coated chicken items in the air fryer (you can do a dual-stack if you have the extra rack device).
5. Establish air fryer at 350 levels & insert baskets.
6. Cook for 16 mins for a solitary layer or 18 minutes for a double layer.
7. Remove & sprinkle with salt.

8. Offer along with a dish of soup & some ranch clothing for dipping.

Nutrition Info:

- Calories: 630 kcal; Fat: 31g; Carbs:52g; Proteins: 36g

Whole30 Lemon Pepper Chicken In The Air Fryer

Ingredients:

- A little salt
- Some pepper
- A handful; of black peppercorns
- 1 teaspoon of garlic puree
- 1 tablespoon of garlic seasoning
- 2 lemons rind
- Juice
- 1 chicken breast

Directions:

1. Preheat your air fryer to about 356°F.
2. Spread a large sheet of foil on your countertop and add the seasoning and the lemon rind.
3. Trim off all the fat on your chicken breast. You can easily do that on a chopping board. You should also remove all the bones if any.
4. Season both sides of the chicken breast with pepper and salt. After that, you can now coat both sides of the chicken breast with the chicken seasoning.
5. Place it in the silver foil sheet and rub it well so that it is fully seasoned.
6. Seal it up tightly, to lock the flavor into it. Flatten it out with a rolling pin to release more flavor.
7. Place it in the air fryer for up to 15 minutes. Sometimes, it does not take up to 15 minutes before it gets done. So, you need to be checking it at intervals.
8. When it is done, bring it out and leave it for a few minutes to cool down before you serve it.

Nutrition Info:

- Total Calories: 140Kcal Carbohydrates: 24g Protein: 13g Fat: 2g Cholesterol: 32mg Sodium: 64mg Potassium: 483mg Fiber: 6g Sugar: 5g Calcium: 100mg Iron: 3mg Vitamin A: 115mg Vitamin C: 116mg

Carrot Ginger Soup

Servings: 4 | Cooking Time: 20 Minutes

Ingredients:

- 1 tablespoon olive oil
- 1 medium yellow onion, chopped
- 3 cups fat-free chicken broth
- 1 pound carrots, peeled and chopped
- 1 tablespoon fresh grated ginger
- ¼ cup fat-free sour cream
- Salt and pepper

Directions:

1. Heat the oil in a large saucepan over medium heat.
2. Add the onions and sauté for 5 minutes until softened.
3. Stir in the broth, carrots, and ginger then cover and bring to a boil
4. Reduce heat and simmer for 20 minutes.
5. Stir in the sour cream then remove from heat.
6. Blend using an immersion blender until smooth and creamy.
7. Season with salt and pepper to taste then serve hot.

Nutrition Info:

• Calories 120, Total Fat 3.6g, Saturated Fat 1g, Total Carbs 17.2g, Net Carbs 13.6g

Buffalo Cauliflower Wings

Servings: 6 | Cooking Time: 30 Minutes

Ingredients:

• 1 tablespoon almond flour
• 1 medium head of cauliflower
• 1 ½ teaspoon salt
• 4 tablespoons hot sauce
• 1 tablespoon olive oil

Directions:

1. Switch on the air fryer, insert fryer basket, grease it with olive oil, then shut with its lid, set the fryer at 400 degrees F and preheat for 5 minutes.
2. Meanwhile, cut cauliflower into bite-size florets and set aside.
3. Place flour in a large bowl, whisk in salt, oil and hot sauce until combined, add cauliflower florets and toss until combined.
4. Open the fryer, add cauliflower florets in it in a single layer, close with its lid and cook for 15 minutes until nicely golden and crispy, shaking halfway through the frying.
5. When air fryer beeps, open its lid, transfer cauliflower florets onto a serving plate and keep warm.
6. Cook the remaining cauliflower florets in the same manner and serve.

Nutrition Info:

• Calories: 48 CalCarbs: 1 gFat: 4 gProtein: 1 gFiber: 0.5 g

Blistered Shishito Peppers

Servings: 1 | Cooking Time: 10 Minutes

Ingredients:

• 1 lb. Shishito peppers washed as well as patted dry.
• 1 tsp. sesame oil.
• 1/4 tsp. coconut amino.
• Kosher salt.
• sesame seeds

Directions:

1. Include the peppers to the basket of your air fryer. liberally spray with olive oil food preparation spray.
2. Prepare at 350F for 10 minutes, trembling the basket midway. Food preparation time will depend on the size of your peppers and also how "done" you desire them.
3. Add the peppers to a bowl and throw with the sesame oil and coconut amino.

Nutrition Info:

• Calories: 32 kcal; Carbs: 5g; Protein:0g; Fat: 1g

Sweet Potato Chips

Servings: 4 | Cooking Time: 10 Minutes

Ingredients:

• 2 large sweet potatoes, cut into strips 25 mm thick
• 15 ml of oil
• 10g of salt
• 2g black pepper
• 2g of paprika
• 2g garlic powder
• 2g onion powder

Directions:

1. Cut the sweet potatoes into strips 25 mm thick.
2. Preheat the air fryer for a few minutes.
3. Add the cut sweet potatoes in a large bowl and mix with the oil until the potatoes are all evenly coated.
4. Sprinkle salt, black pepper, paprika, garlic powder and onion powder. Mix well.
5. Place the French fries in the preheated baskets and cook for 10 minutes at 205°C. Be sure to shake the baskets halfway through cooking.

Nutrition Info:

• Calories: 123 Cal Carbs: 2 g Fat: 11 g Protein: 4 g Fiber: 0 g

Lemony Yogurt Pound Cake

Ingredients:

• 1/4 teaspoon of fine salt
• 1/4 cup of low-fat milk
• 1/4 cup of extra-virgin olive oil
• 1 1/2 cups of white whole wheat flour
• 1/2 cup of plain low-fat Greek yogurt
• 1/2 teaspoon of pure vanilla extract
• Nonstick baking spray, for coating the loaf pan
• 2 teaspoons of baking powder
• Finely grated zest of 1 lemon
• 2 large egg whites
• 1 large egg

Directions:

1. Preheat your air fryer to 350 degrees F. Coat a loaf pan with baking spray.
2. Whisk the salt together with baking powder and flour. Add the yogurt to the whole eggs, egg whites, vanilla, olive oil, and milk. Whisk the mixture thoroughly until the mixture is smoothly blended.
3. Add the flour mixture to the egg mixture and stir them

together.

4. Bake the new mixture in your air fryer for about 50 minutes. Insert the cake tester. If it comes out clean, it means the cake is done.

5. Allow it to cool before you divide and serve it.

Nutrition Info:

- Calories: 254 Total Fat: 8g Cholesterol: 25mg Sodium: 195mg Carbohydrates: 38g Dietary Fiber: 3g Protein: 6g

Two-bean Beef Chili

Ingredients:

- 2 tablespoons of olive oil
- 1 onion, chopped
- 3 stalks of celery, diced
- 1 ½ pound of ground beef (ideally 85% lean)
- 3 tablespoons of the chili powder blend
- 1 teaspoon of garlic powder
- 1 teaspoon of kosher salt
- 1 can of pinto or pink beans
- 1 can of black beans
- 1 can of crushed or pureed tomatoes
- 2 tablespoons of white vinegar
- Grated cheese, sour cream, chopped red onions, and hot sauce to be used for toppings

Directions:

1. Heat the oil over medium-low heat. You can add celery, onions, and sauté to the oil and air fry until the ingredients have turned brown in color. This should not exceed 10 minutes.

2. Increase the heat and break the ground into crumbs while it is cooking. Cook the meat until it turns brown. This should happen within 5 minutes of cooking.

3. After that, you should reduce the heat from high to low before you add salt, garlic, and chili. Stir the mixture for 15 seconds before you add the tomatoes and the beans. Continue heating the mixture on low heat until it becomes thicker. This will take about 30 minutes to 45 minutes.

4. Please don't alter the quantities of the ingredients. If you do, you may not get a perfect taste. When you become an expert, you can now begin to tweak the recipe to suit your desire.

5. You can now serve it.

Nutrition Info:

- Calories: 140 Total Fat: 2.6g Sodium: 501mg Potassium:857.7mg Carbohydrates:27.3g Fiber: 7.5g Glucose: 7g Protein: 7.2g Calcium: 600mg Iron: 0.4mg

Spaghetti Squash Alfredo

Servings: 2 | Cooking Time: 15 Minutes

Ingredients:

- ½ large cooked spaghetti squash
- ¼ cup grated vegetarian Parmesan cheese.
- ½ cup shredded Italian blend cheese
- ½ cup low-carb Alfredo sauce
- 2 tbsp. salted butter; melted.
- ¼ tsp. ground peppercorn
- ½ tsp. garlic powder.
- 1 tsp. dried parsley.

Directions:

1. Using a fork, remove the strands of spaghetti squash from the shell. Place into a large bowl with butter and Alfredo sauce. Sprinkle with Parmesan, garlic powder, parsley and peppercorn

2. Pour into a 4-cup round baking dish and top with shredded cheese. Place dish into the air fryer basket. Modify the temperature to 320 Degrees F and set the timer for 15 minutes.

3. When finished, cheese will be golden and bubbling. Serve immediately.

Nutrition Info:

- Calories: 375 Protein: 13.5g Fiber: 4.0g Fat: 24.2g Carbs: 24.1g

Air Fryer Sweet Potato Nachos

Ingredients:

- 1 tablespoon of Freshly Minced Cilantro
- 2 tablespoons of Light Sour Cream
- ½ cup of Shredded Romaine Lettuce
- 4 Cherry tomatoes
- 2/3 cup of Thinly Sliced Radishes
- ¼ cup of Salsa
- ¼ cup of reduced-fat Shredded Cheddar Cheese
- 1 Jalapeno Pepper (split and seeded)
- 1 ½ cup of Frozen Pepper-and-Onion Blend
- 1 nonstick cooking spray
- 1 medium sweet potato

Directions:

1. Cut each of the four cherry tomatoes into four equal parts. Also, slice the sweet potato into 1/8-inch thick chips.

2. Place the potato chips in the air fryer basket and spray it with nonstick cooking spray. Put some of the vegetables on the potato chips with a spoon. Now, place the jalapeno pepper over the vegetables, with the skin side facing up. Spray with the nonstick spray again.

3. Now, you can set the temperature to 375° F and air fry the potato for a third of an hour. By then, the potatoes should be done. Your aim is to make the chips crisp but not soft.

4. Remove the jalapeno pepper and place it in a bowl. Leave it loosely covered for 5 minutes.

5. Lightly sprinkle the cheese on the vegetables and air fry it for just 2 minutes to make the cheese melt. Remove the charred skin of the jalapeno pepper and chop it (pepper).

6. Remove the potatoes and veggies from the air fryer. Place them somewhere and sprinkle the chopped jalapeno pepper on the vegetables.

7. Top the chips of potatoes with some lettuce, tomatoes, radishes, and salsa.Finally, add a dollop of sour cream and cilantro. You can now serve it.

Nutrition Info:

• Calories: 100 Total Fat: 2.5g Phosphorus: 95mg Potassium: 450mg Protein: 4g Total Carbohydrate: 17g Sodium: 180mg Cholesterol: 4mg

Air Fried Salmon Belly

Servings: 2

Ingredients:

• 1-pound salmon belly, skin on, trimmed, sliced into ¾-inch thick sliver
• 2 Tbsp. almond flour, finely milled
• Pinch of sea salt
• Dip
• ¼ tsp. fresh garlic, minced
• ½ cup coconut or palm vinegar
• ¼ cup white onion, minced
• ¼ tsp. fish sauce
• 1 piece bird's eye chili, deseeded, minced
• black pepper to taste

Directions:

1. Preheat Air Fryer to 330 degrees F.
2. Combine palm vinegar, fish sauce, white onion, bird's eye chili, garlic, and pepper in a small bowl. Set aside.
3. Season salmon belly with the mixture. Roll in almond flour.
4. Layer fillet in the Air Fryer's basket. Fry for 5 minutes or until golden brown. Drain on paper towels.
5. Serve with dip or on bed of rice

Nutrition Info:

• Calorie: 129Carbohydrate: 5.35g Fat: 0.8Protein: 11.99g Fiber: 0.3g .

Eggplant Fries

Servings: 4 | Cooking Time: 20 Minutes

Ingredients:

• 1 eggplant, cut into 3-inch pieces
• 1/4 cup water
• 1 tbsp. olive oil
• 4 tbsps. cornstarch
• Sea salt

Directions:

1. Adjust the temperature of the air fryer to 390°Ft.
2. Mix the eggplant, water, oil, and cornstarch in a bowl.

3. Place the eggplant fries in the air fryer basket, and air fry them for 20 minutes. Serve warm.

Nutrition Info:

• Calories: 113.2 kcal; Fat: 7.2g; Protein: 1.9g; Carbs: 12.3g

Coconut Pie

Servings: 6 | Cooking Time: 45 Minutes

Ingredients:

• 1/2 cup coconut flour
• 1/2 cup erythritol sweetener
• 1 cup shredded coconut, unsweetened, divided
• 1/4 cup butter, unsalted
• 1 1/2 teaspoon vanilla extract, unsweetened
• 2 eggs, pastured
• 1 1/2 cups milk, low-fat, unsweetened
• ¼ cup shredded coconut, toasted

Directions:

1. Switch on the air fryer, insert fryer basket, grease it with olive oil, then shut with its lid, set the fryer at 350 degrees F and preheat for 5 minutes.
2. Meanwhile, place all the ingredients in a bowl and whisk until well blended and smooth batter comes together.
3. Take a 6-inches pie pan, grease it oil, then pour in the prepared batter and smooth the top.
4. Open the fryer, place the pie pan in it, close with its lid and cook for 45 minutes until pie has set and inserted a toothpick into the pie slide out clean.
5. When air fryer beeps, open its lid, take out the pie pan and let it cool.
6. Garnish the pie with toasted coconut, then cut into slices and serve.

Nutrition Info:

• Calories: 236 CalCarbs: 16 gFat: 16 gProtein: 3 gFiber: 2 g

Sweet And Sour Chicken

Ingredients:

• basmati rice to serve
• 2 teaspoons of vegetable oil
• 2 tablespoons of pineapple juice
• 2 spring onions (should be sliced into pieces
• 2 finely chopped garlic 2 cloves
• 2 chicken breasts 2 (should be cut into bite-sized pieces)
• 100g of pineapple chunks
• 1 tablespoon of tomato ketchup
• 1 tablespoon of dark soy sauce
• 1 tablespoon of corn flour
• 1 finely chopped piece of ginger
• 1 diced red pepper
• 1 diced green pepper
• 1 ½ tablespoon of rice vinegar
• ½tablespoon of soft light brown sugar

Directions:

1. Heat the vegetable oil in a pan. The next step is to cook the chicken for 5 minutes. Now, air fry the mixture of peppers and onions for another 5 minutes. By then, the mixture will be charred. Add the ginger and garlic to the charred mixture and cook it for another 1 minute.
2. Mix the cornflour together with vinegar, soy, and pineapple juice. Stir them until the mixture is even.
3. You can now add 100ml of water and ketchup to the mix. Pour the mixture into a pan and add the chicken. Cook the mixture for 5 minutes before you turn the chicken over. Then, you can cook it for another 5 minutes. By then, the sauce will be thick and the chicken will be done.
4. Stir in the pineapple chinks in the last 2 minutes of cooking.
5. Serve the chicken along with the basmati rice.

Nutrition Info:

• • Total Fat: 9.7g • Salt: 1.4g • Protein: 39g • Fiber: 5.7g • Carbohydrates: 69.9g • Calories: 5

Vegetarian Spinach Rolls

Ingredients:

• Cooking spray
• 4ounces off at-free cottage cheese
• 3eggs
• 2½ounces of onions
• 2ounces of carrot
• 16ounces of frozen spinach leaves
• 1teaspoon of curry powder
• 1teaspoon of salt
• 1teaspoon of pepper
• 1ounce of low-fat mozzarella cheese
• 1clovesgarlic
• ¾cup of parsley
• ¼teaspoon of chili flakes

Directions:

1. The first thing is to preheat your air fryer to 400 degrees F while you allow the spinach to thaw. Make sure you squeeze out the little water left in the spinach. While some people will microwave the spinach for a few minutes to facilitate things, we prefer to leave it to thaw on its own. The choice is totally yours.
2. Mix the pepper, garlic, half of the salt, mozzarella, and 2 eggs together with the spinach.
3. Spray your air fryer basket with cooking spray. Put the spinach mixture in the basket and bake it for about 15 minutes. Then, remove it to allow it cool.
4. Grate the carrots and chop the onions and parsley. Apply some cooking spray on your skillet before you fry the onions on it for about 60 seconds. You can now add the grated carrots and chopped parsley to the fried onions and allow the mixture to simmer for 2 minutes.
5. Pour the other half of the salt in a bowl and add pepper, chili, curry, and cottage cheese to it. Mix them up until they are even. Add egg to the onions-parsley mixture.

6. Spread the spinach on a flat surface and spread the filling/mixture on it.
7. Roll the spinach up with the fillings inside it and bake it for another 25 minutes.
8. When it is done, allow it to cool down for 10 minutes before you cut it into slices. You can now serve it as slices.

Nutrition Info:

• Vitamin C: 46.1mg Vitamin A: 8770IU Total Fat: 10.4g Sodium: 695mg Protein: 27.3g Potassium: 2489.3mg Iron 5mg Fiber: 5.1g Cholesterol: 326.7mg Carbohydrates: 19.6g Calories: 310 Calcium: 419mg

Air-fryer Onion Strings

Servings: 3-4

Ingredients:

• 2 cups buttermilk
• 1 piece, whole white onion, halved, julienned
• 2 cups almond flour, finely milled
• ½ tsp. cayenne pepper
• Pinch of sea salt
• Pinch of black pepper to taste

Directions:

1. Preheat Air Fryer to 330 degrees F.
2. Soak onion strings in buttermilk for 1 hour before frying. Drain.
3. Meanwhile, mix almond flour, cayenne pepper, salt and pepper in a bowl. Coat onion strings with flour mixture.
4. Layer onions in Air fryer basket. Fry until golden brown and crisp. Drain on paper towels. Season with salt. Serve.

Nutrition Info:

• Calorie: 150Carbohydrate: 13g Fat: 17g Protein: 2g Fiber: 1g

Low-fat Roasties

Ingredients:

• 800g of roasting potatoes
• 1 garlic clove
• 200ml of vegetable stock
• 2 tablespoons of olive oil

Directions:

1. Slice the garlic and divide potatoes into four equal parts.
2. Preheat your air fryer to 392 degrees F.
3. Put the potatoes and garlic together and coat them with half of the olive oil.
4. Pour the stock into the mix.
5. Air fry them for about 50 minutes before you turn them over, brush them with the remaining olive oil.
6. Cook them for another 15 minutes. By then, both of them would have turned brown in color and the stock will be absorbed. Let the potatoes cool for 5 minutes before you serve it.

Nutrition Info:

- Calories: 201 Total Fat: 6g Carbohydrates: 35g Fiber: 3g Protein: 5g Salt: 0.2g

Ceviche-stuffed Avocado Halves

Servings: 6 | Cooking Time: None

Ingredients:

- 2 lemons, juiced
- 2 limes, juiced
- 3 to 4 drops liquid stevia extract
- 6 ounces cooked shrimp, chopped
- ¼ cup diced seedless cucumber
- ¼ cup diced tomato
- 1 jalapeno, seeded and minced (optional)
- 2 tablespoons fresh chopped cilantro
- 1 tablespoon olive oil
- Salt
- 3 medium avocados

Directions:

1. Whisk together the lemon juice, lime juice, and liquid stevia in a medium bowl.
2. Toss in the shrimp then cover and chill for 20 minutes.
3. Drain the shrimp and toss with the cucumber, tomato, jalapeno, and cilantro.
4. Drizzle with olive oil then season with salt and toss well to combine.
5. Cut the avocados in half and remove the pits.
6. Spoon ¼ cup of the shrimp mixture onto each half to serve.

Nutrition Info:

- Calories 270, Total Fat 22.6g, Saturated Fat 4.7g, Total Carbs 11.2g, Net Carbs 4.1g, Protein 8.7g, Sugar 1.4g, Fiber 7.1g, Sodium 106mg

Unstuffed Cabbage

Ingredients:

- 1-tablespoon olive oil
- 1 small onion, chopped
- 1½ cups chopped green cabbage
- 16 precooked frozen meatballs
- 1 cup frozen cooked rice
- 2 tomatoes, chopped
- ½ teaspoon dried marjoram
- Pinch salt
- Freshly ground black pepper

Directions:

1. In a 6-inch metal bowl, combine the oil and the onion. Bake for 2 to 4 minutes or until the onion is crisp and tender.
2. Add the cabbage, meatballs, rice, tomatoes, marjoram, salt, and pepper, and stir.
3. Bake for 12 to 16 minutes, stirring once during cooking time, until the meatballs are hot, the rice is warmed, and the vegetables are tender.

Nutrition Info:

- Calories: 453; Total Fat: 20g; Saturated Fat: 7g; Cholesterol: 47mg; Sodium: 590mg; Carbohydrates: 51g; Fiber: 4g; Protein: 25g

Air Fried Veggie Quesadillas

Ingredients:

- Cooking spray
- 4 sprouted whole-grain flour tortillas
- 4 ounces reduced-fat sharp Cheddar cheese, shredded (about 1 cup)
- 2 tablespoons of chopped fresh cilantro
- 2 ounces of plain reduced-fat Greek yogurt
- 1/4 teaspoon of ground cumin
- 1/2 cup of drained refrigerated pico de gallo
- 1 teaspoon of lime zest plus 1 Tbsp. fresh juice (from 1 lime)
- 1 cup of sliced zucchini
- 1 cup of sliced red bell pepper
- 1 cup of no-salt-added canned black beans, drained and rinsed

Directions:

1. Sprinkle 2 tablespoons of shredded cheese over half of each tortilla. After that, you can add cheese on tortilla. Also, add black beans, slices of zucchini, and a quarter cup of red pepper slices on the tortilla as well.
2. Sprinkle the remaining cheese on the tortilla. Now, you can fold the tortilla in the shape of half moon. They will now become quesadillas. We hope you understand that quesadillas are tortillas with fillings.
3. Coat the quesadillas with cooking spray and secure them with toothpicks.
4. Coat the air fryer basket with cooking spray. Then, you can place the quesadillas in the basket. Cook them at 400 degrees F until they turn golden brown and crispy. This should happen after about 10 minutes of cooking. Remember to turn the quesadillas over after 5 minutes. You can air fry all the quesadillas at once or in two batches.
5. While the quesadillas are being cooked, mix the cumin, lime juice, lime zest, and yogurt together in a bowl.
6. You need to cut each of the quesadillas into wedges before you serve them. It is also necessary to sprinkle cilantro on them. Serve each of them with a tablespoon of cumin and 2 tablespoons of Pico de Gallo

Nutrition Info:

- Calories: 291 Fat: 8g Saturated Fat: 4g Unsaturated Fat: 3g Protein: 17g Carbohydrates: 36g Fiber: 8g Sodium: 518mg Calcium: 30% DV Potassium: 6% DV

Air Fried Apple Chips

Ingredients:

- Cooking spray
- 2 teaspoons of canola oil
- 1/4 cup of plain low-fat Greek yogurt
- 1 teaspoon of honey
- 1 teaspoon of ground cinnamon
- 1 tablespoon of almond butter
- 1 apple

Directions:

1. Slice the apple into thin slices.
2. Mix the slices of apple with oil and cinnamon, before you toss them together for even coating.
3. Apply cooking spray on your air fryer basket.
4. Place the slices of apple in the air fryer basket. Don't place more than 8 slices on a single layer.
5. Cook the apple at 375 degrees F for 12 minutes. Ensure you rearrange the slices of apple after every 4 minutes. It is possible that the apple chips are not crispy enough when you remove them from your air fryer. They will become even crispier as they cool.
6. If there are slices of apple left, you can do the same thing to them.
7. Mix the honey, almond butter and yogurt together evenly. Add a dollop of the sauce to every serving of the apple chips.

Nutrition Info:

- Unsaturated Fat 2g Sodium: 187mg Saturated Fat 1g Protein: 1g Potassium: 6% DV Fiber: 3g Fat: 3 Carbohydrates: 17g Calories: 104 Calcium: 3% DV

Fried Squash Flowers

Servings: 3 | Cooking Time: 8 Minutes

Ingredients:

- 2-1/2 lbs. rinsed squash flowers
- 1 cup coconut flour, finely milled
- Pinch of sea salt, to taste
- raisin vinegar for garnish, optional

Directions:

1. Adjust the temperature of the Air Fryer to 330ºF.
2. Season squash blossoms with salt. Dredge into coconut flour.
3. Layer breaded blossoms in the air fryer basket. Fry for 2 minutes or until golden brown. Drain on paper towels.
4. Stack cooked squash blossoms in the middle of plates. Sprinkle raisin vinegar. Serve.

Nutrition Info:

- Calories: 5g; Carbs: 1g; Fat: 0g; Protein: 0g

Loaded Potatoes In An Air Fryer

Ingredients:

- 1/8 teaspoon of Kosher salt
- 2 tablespoons of reduced-fat sour cream
- ½ ounce reduced-fat Cheddar cheese
- 1 ½ tablespoon of chopped fresh chives
- 2 center-cut bacon slices
- 1 teaspoon of olive oil
- 11 ounces of potatoes

Directions:

1. Get the Cheddar cheese shredded finely. You should get up to 2 tablespoons of it. Before placing the potatoes in the air fryer basket, toss them in oil to coat them up.
2. Set the temperature of your air fryer to 350 degrees F and cook the potatoes for about 25 minutes. You should stir it occasionally. After about 25 minutes, the potatoes will be tender.
3. Cook the bacon in a skillet over medium heat until it becomes crispy. That should take only 7 minutes.
4. After that, you can crumble the bacon. Now, you can place potatoes on a serving platter and crush them.
5. Mix them in the crumbled bacon. Then, add some chives, cheese, sour cream, and salt. You can now serve the meal.

Nutrition Info:

- Potassium: Less than 1g Calcium: Less than 1g Sodium: 287mg Fiber: 4g Carbohydrate: 26g Protein: 7g Saturated Fat: 3g Unsaturated Fat: 2g Calories: 199

Air Fried Calzones

Ingredients:

- Cooking spray
- 6 ounces of fresh prepared whole-wheat pizza dough
- 3 ounces of baby spinach leaves (about 3 cups)
- 2 ounces of shredded rotisserie chicken breast (about 1/3 cup)
- 1/4 cup of finely chopped red onion (you can get the quantity from 1 small onion)
- 1/3 cup of lower-sodium marinara sauce
- 1 teaspoon of olive oil
- 1 1/2 ounces of pre-shredded part-skim mozzarella cheese (about 6 Tbsp.)

Directions:

1. The first step is to heat the oil in a nonstick skillet. Set the heat to medium-high for that.
2. Add onion to the oil and cook them together, but make sure you stir the onions while it is cooking. Do this for just 2 minutes or until the onion is tender.
3. Add spinach and cook it until it has wilted. This should happen within 2 minutes of cooking.
4. Add the spinach to the chicken and marinara, and stir them together.
5. Divide the dough into four equal portions. Coat each

piece with some flour. Then, roll each of them into a 6-inch circle. Place ¼ of the spinach mixture on half of each dough circle.

6. Add ¼ of the cheese to each half of the dough circle as well.

7. Fold the dough over the filling to form the shape of half moon. Crimp their edges to keep them sealed.

8. Coat the calzones with cooking spray and place them in your air fryer basket.

9. Cook them at 325 degrees F for about 12 minutes before turning them over. Cook them for another 8 minutes. They should be golden brown in color by then. You can now serve them.

Nutrition Info:

• Unsaturated Fat: 7g Sodium: 710mg Saturated Fat:3g Protein: 21g Potassium: 3% DV Fiber: 5g Fat: 12g Carbohydrates: 44g Calories: 348 Calcium: 21% DV

Pan-seared Salmon With Kale And Apple Salad

Ingredients:

• Four 5-ounce center-cut salmon fillets
• 3 tablespoons of fresh lemon juice
• 3 tablespoons of olive oil
• Kosher salt
• 1 bunch of kale
• 1/4 cup of dates
• 1 apple
• 1/4 cup of finely grated pecorino
• 3 tablespoons of toasted slivered almonds
• Freshly ground black pepper
• 4 whole wheat dinner rolls

Directions:

1. Remove the ribs of the kale leaves and slice them thinly.

2. Allow the salmon to thaw before you do anything to it. Whisk ¼ teaspoon of salt, 2 tablespoons of olive oil, and lemon juice together. Add the kale leaves to the mixture and toss them together. After that, leave the mixture for 10 minutes.

3. On the other hand, slice the dates and cut the apple into matchsticks. Add almonds, cheese, apple pieces, and dates to the kale mixture. Season it with the pepper and toss it well.

4. Sprinkle some pepper and ½ teaspoon of salt on the salmon fillets.

5. Heat the oil before you coat the salmon fillets with it. Air fry the fillets for 4 minutes, until they turn golden brown. Turn them over and fry for another 4 minutes. You can now serve the fillets with kale and apple salad.

Nutrition Info:

• Calories: 620 Total Fat: 36g Cholesterol: 85mg Sodium: 730mg Carbohydrates: 40g Dietary Fiber: 7g Protein: 39g

Air Fryer Sweet Potato Tots

Ingredients:

• Nonstick cooking spray
• ¾ cup of ketchup (the one without salt)
• 1 ¼ teaspoon of kosher salt
• 1/8 teaspoon of garlic powder
• 1 tablespoon of potato starch
• 2 small sweet potatoes

Directions:

1. Peel and boil the potatoes in a pot until they are tender. This should not take more than a quarter of an hour. Transfer the boiled potatoes to a plate and leave for 15 minutes to cool.

2. Get a medium bowl. Grate the potatoes into the bowl. After that, you can add the grated potatoes to the same bowl with 1 teaspoon of salt, garlic powder, and potato starch. Then, toss them together.

3. Mold the mixture into about 6 tot-shaped cylinders.

4. Coat your air fryer basket with cooking spray. After that, you can place each of the tots in the air fryer basket and spray them with a cooking spray as well.

5. Place them in your air fryer and set the temperature to 400°F. Let it cook for about 13 minutes. You should stop and turn them over after 7 minutes.

6. When they are done, they will be lightly brown in color. Remove the tots and sprinkle the remaining 1/8 teaspoon of salt on them. You can then serve them with ketchup immediately.

Nutrition Info:

• Total Calories: 78 Potassium: very low quantity Calcium: very low Sodium: 335mg Sugars: 8g Fiber: 2g Carbohydrates: 19g Protein: 1g

Stuffed Portabella Mushrooms

Servings: 2

Ingredients:

• 2 dozen fresh portabella mushrooms, minced
• 2 tsp. olive oil, add more for drizzling/greasing
• Filling
• 1 Tbsp. olive oil
• 1 onion, minced
• 2 garlic cloves, grated
• 3 Tbsp. butter, unsalted
• ¼ cup apple cider vinegar
• 2 Tbsp. fresh parsley, minced
• ¼ cup roasted cashew nuts, crushed
• ¼-cup cheddar cheese, reduced fat, grated
• ¼ cup Parmesan cheese, grated
• Pinch of sea salt
• Pinch of black pepper to taste

Directions:

1. Preheat Air Fryer to 330 degrees F.

2. Meanwhile, in a pan heat the oil. Sauté onion and garlic

for 2 minutes or until translucent and fragrant. Stir in butter, almonds, mushrooms stems, salt, and pepper. Cook for 3 minutes or until mushrooms turn brown in color.

3. Pour vinegar. Cook until the liquid is reduced. Stir in nuts and Parmesan cheese. Allow mixture to cool.

4. Spoon mixture into mushroom caps. Layer mushrooms in the prepared baking dish. Place inside the Air fryer basket. Cook for 20 minutes. Serve.

Nutrition Info:
- Calorie: 129Carbohydrate: 5.35g Fat: 0.8g Protein: 11.99g Fiber: 0.3g

Air-fryer Cauliflower Gnocchi With Marinara Dipping Sauce

Ingredients:
- 3 tablespoons of extra-virgin olive oil, divided
- 2 tablespoons of chopped fresh flat-leaf parsley
- 2 packs of frozen cauliflower gnocchi
- 1 cup of reduced-sodium marinara sauce
- ½ cup of grated Parmesan cheese

Directions:
1. Start the process by preheating your air fryer to 375 degrees F. Mix 1 pack of gnocchi with 1 ½ tablespoon of oil and 2 tablespoons of parmesan together evenly.
2. Spray your air fryer basket with cooking spray before you place the gnocchi mixture in it.
3. Cook it for 3 minutes and turn it over before you cook for another 2 minutes.
4. Repeat the process with the second pack of gnocchi.
5. When it is done, you should sprinkle parsley and the remaining ¼ cup of Parmesan on the gnocchi.
6. It is best served with marinara.

Nutrition Info:
- Vitamin C: 3mg Total Fat: 9.3g Sodium: 163mg Saturated Fat: 1.9g Protein: 3g Potassium: 85mg Magnesium: 2mg Iron: 1mg Fiber: 3.6g Cholesterol: 4mg Carbohydrates: 14.1g Calories: 159 Calcium: 69mg

Veggie Bowl

Servings: 3 | Cooking Time: 30 Minutes

Ingredients:
- 4 cups Brussel sprouts
- 6 cups sweet potato
- 2 tsp garlic powder
- 2 tbsps. Low sodium soy sauce
- Cooking spray

Directions:
1. Place the sweet potatoes in the air-fryer. Add a light layer of oil for tossing.
2. Top it with 1 tsp of garlic powder and toss.
3. Set the temperature to 400 F and cook for 15 minutes. Toss after 5 minutes.

4. Transfer the Brussels sprouts to the cooking basket and spray a layer of oil and the remaining garlic powder. Toss them well and cook at 400 F for 5 minutes.
5. Drizzle some soy sauce and shake to coat the vegetables evenly.
6. Set to the same temperature and cook for 5 minutes. Check it when it hits 2 minutes and toss the contents.
7. cooking time will depend on the vegetable. Once the vegetables are done, they will be soft and brown.

Nutrition Info:
- Calories: 445 kcal; Fat: 8g; Carbs: 86g; Protein: 17g

Air Fryer Tofu

Servings: 1 | Cooking Time: 5 Minutes

Ingredients:
- 16 oz block added company tofu.
- 2 tbsps. low salt soy sauce.
- 1 tbsp. additional virgin olive oil.
- 1 tsp diced garlic.
- 1/2 tsp sriracha.

Directions:
1. Press Tofu-Use a tofu press, or line a plate with paper towels. Place a block of tofu ahead as well as place more paper towels on the top of the tofu so that the tofu is sandwiched between paper towels. Place a heavy pan on top of the tofu with 4 hefty containers in addition to the pan. Enable to sit for thirty minutes.
2. When tofu is pushed piece into 1-inch dices.
3. Mix soy sauce, olive oil, garlic, as well as sriracha in a small bowl. Turn tofu halfway with marinating time to make sure all sides saturate up the sauce.
4. Set tofu in air fryer basket in a single layer. Don't jam-pack. Cook for 10 mins at 375 F. Toss at the 5-minute mark.

Nutrition Info:
- Calories:115 kcal; Fat: 4g; Carbs: 2g; Proteins: 7g

Air-fried Spicy Chicken Wing Drumettes

Ingredients:
- Cooking spray
- 3/8 teaspoon of crushed red pepper
- 3 tablespoons of honey
- 2 tablespoons of unsalted chicken stock
- 2 tablespoons of chopped unsalted roasted peanuts
- 10 large chicken drumettes
- 1/4 cup of rice vinegar
- 1 tablespoon of toasted sesame oil
- 1 tablespoon of lower-sodium soy sauce
- 1 finely chopped garlic clove
- 1 tablespoon of chopped fresh chives

Directions:
1. The first step is to place the chicken in the basket of

your air fryer. Spray cooking spray on them. Cook them for about 25 minutes at the temperature of 400 degrees F. By then, the chicken will be crispy. Remember to turn them over half way into the cooking time.

2. While the chicken is being cooked, mix the garlic, crushed red pepper, soy sauce, oil, stock, honey, and vinegar together in a skillet.

3. Heat them with medium-high heat, for the mixture to simmer. Wait until the sauce thickens slightly. It will feel like syrup. This will happen within only 6 minutes of heating.

4. Now, you can place the chicken drumettes in a bowl, and add the honey syrup mixture to the drumettes.

5. Toss them to get the chicken coated.

6. Sprinkle them with chives and peanuts before they are served. This dish is best eaten hot or warm.

Nutrition Info:

• Unsaturated Fat: 21g Sodium: 409mg Saturated Fat: 7g Protein: 25g Potassium: 2% DV Fiber: 1g Fat: 30g Calories: 488 Calcium: 1% DV

Crispy Baked Tofu

Servings: 4 | Cooking Time: 25 Minutes

Ingredients:

• 1 (14-ounce) block extra-firm tofu
• 1 tablespoon olive oil
• 1 tablespoon cornstarch
• ½ teaspoon garlic powder
• Salt and pepper

Directions:

1. Lay some paper towels out on a flat surface.

2. Cut the tofu into slices up to about ½-inch thick and lay them out.

3. Cover the tofu with another paper towel and place a cutting board on top.

4. Let the tofu drain for 10 to 15 minutes.

5. Preheat the oven to 400°F and line a baking sheet with foil or parchment.

6. Cut the tofu into cubes and place in a large bowl.

7. Toss with the olive oil, cornstarch, and garlic powder, salt and pepper until coated.

8. Spread on the baking sheet and bake for 10 minutes.

9. Flip the tofu and bake for another 10 to 15 minutes until crisp. Serve hot.

Nutrition Info:

• Calories 140 Total Fat 8.7g,Saturated Fat 1.1g, Total Carbs 2.1g, Net Carbs 2g, Protein.7g, Sugar 0.1g, Fiber 0.1g, Sodium 23mg

Air Fried Beet Chips

Ingredients:

• 3/4 teaspoon of kosher salt
• 3 medium-size red beets
• 2 teaspoons of canola oil
• 1/4 teaspoon of black pepper

Directions:

1. Peel the beets and cut them into 1/8-inch-thick slices.

2. Add oil, pepper, and salt to the beets, and toss the mixture together.

3. Divide the beets into two portions and cook one portion first.

4. Cook half portion in your air fryer at 320 degrees F for about 30 minutes. Don't forget to shake your air fryer basket every 5 minutes.

5. Do the same with the second portion. You can now serve them in four plates for different people.

Nutrition Info:

• Unsaturated Fat: 2g Sodium: 48mg Saturated Fat: 0g Protein: 1g Potassium: 4% DV Fiber: 2g Fat: 2g Carbohydrates: 6g Calories: 47 Calcium: 1% DV

Non-gluten Free Diabetic Cheesecakes

Ingredients:

• 4 eggs
• 1 cup of sour cream
• 1 tablespoon of vanilla
• 3 tablespoons of flour
• 5 packages of softened cream cheese. That should be about 8 oz.
• A pair of honey graham cracker crusts
• Crust

Directions:

1. Preheat your air fryer to about 325 degrees. While still in their tins, put the graham cracker crusts in the fryer and warm them for about 3 minutes.

2. Mix the vanilla, flour, and cream cheese all together in a bowl. It often produces better results if you do the mixing with your bare hands. So, do just that. Mix it until the mixture softens evenly. You can now add some sour cream and mix it again.

3. This time you don't have to use your hands. You can mix it with either your spoon or a whisker. Break and add the eggs, and continue whisking it. You may want to break the eggs one at a time, but make sure you keep whisking it as you break each of the eggs.

4. You can now pour the mixture into the two crusts. Pour an equal amount into each of the crusts and pour it gently to avoid splashing it. Bake the cheesecake for up to 50 minutes. You may set a timer for this. After 50 minutes, you may check it. If it is not yet done, you can keep checking it every 10 minutes. When it is done, the top will be solid, and it will have a golden-brown color.

5. Remove it and allow it to cool down to room temperature.

6. Remove the aluminum tins, and then you can cut it and add toppings before you serve it.

Nutrition Info:

• 102 calories Total Fat: 1.5g Saturated Fat: 2g Protein: 15g Dietary Fiber: 1g Total Carbohydrate: 4g Sodium: 170mg Cholesterol: 106mg

Tuna Steaks

Servings: 1

Ingredients:

• 2 pieces bone-in tuna steaks
• Pinch of salt
• 1 Tbsp. olive oil
• Garnish:
• 1 Tbsp. homemade garlic and parsley butter, divided
• 2 Tbsp. toasted garlic flakes, divided
• ½ small lemon, cut into wedges

Directions:

1. Preheat Air Fryer to 330 degrees F.
2. Season tuna steaks with salt.
3. Layer tuna inside the Air Fryer basket. Fry for 2 minutes on each side. Transfer on a plate.
4. To assemble, place steaks in each plate. Spread parsley and garlic butter. Serve with lemon wedges.

Nutrition Info:

• Calorie: 120Carbohydrate: 0gFat: 1g Protein: 27g Fiber: 0g

Quick Fry Chicken With Cauliflower And Water Chestnuts

Servings: 2-3

Ingredients:

• For the quick fry
• 1½ pounds chicken thigh fillets, diced
• 1 piece, small red bell pepper, julienned
• 1 piece, thumb-sized ginger, grated
• 2 Tbsp. olive oil
• 1 clove, large garlic, minced
• 2 stalks, large leeks, minced
• 1 can, 5 oz. water chestnuts, quartered
• 1 head, small cauliflower, cut into bite-sized florets
• ¾ cups chicken stock, low sodium
• Seasonings
• 1 tsp. stevia
• 1 Tbsp. fish sauce
• ½ Tbsp. cornstarch, dissolved in
• 4 Tbsp. water
• Pinch of salt
• Pinch of black pepper, to taste
• Garnish:

• Leeks, minced
• 1 piece, large lime, cut into 6 wedges

Directions:

1. Preheat Air Fryer to 330 degrees F.
2. Pour olive oil in a pan. Swirl pan to coat. Sauté garlic, ginger, and leeks for 2 minutes. Set aside. Add in water chestnuts, cauliflower, red bell pepper, and chicken broth. Stir well. Cook for 15 minutes.
3. Meanwhile, put the chicken in the Air fryer basket. Fry until seared and golden brown.
4. Add in seasoning into the pan. Stir and cook until the juice thickens.
5. Ladle 1 portion of quick fry veggies and chicken, Garnish with leeks and lemon wedges on the side. Serve.

Nutrition Info:

• Calorie: 220Carbohydrate: 13.6g Fat: 9Protein: 30.5gFiber: 3.8g

Cinnamon Honey Glazed Air Fryer Sweet Potato Bites

Servings: 2 | Cooking Time: 20 Minutes

Ingredients:

• 3 medium Sweet Potatoes
• 1 tbsp Olive Oil Bonus Virgin
• 2 tbsps. Raw Honey Resident
• 2 tsps. Cinnamon

Directions:

1. Wash and peel sweet potatoes. Then dice them.
2. In a large mixing bowl, include oil, honey, as well as cinnamon and toss them until evenly coated.
3. Include wonderful potatoes to the air fryer as well as a chef on 400 for 20-25 mins. Relying on the size of your air fryer, you might need to split the sweet potatoes in half as well as prepare one batch at once.
4. Wonderful potatoes must be crunchy on the outside and soft on the inside as soon as done.
5. Remove from the air fryer and also let the sweet potatoes rest for 5 mins.
6. Serve.

Nutrition Info:

• Calories: 176.1 kcal; Fat: 7.2g; Carbs: 28.8g; Proteins: 1.1g

Crispy Pork Belly Crack

Ingredients:

- ½ teaspoon of pepper
- 1 teaspoon of sea salt
- 1 lb of raw pork belly strips

Directions:

1. Start by slicing the pork belly strips. The idea is to cut the pork into sizes that can be chewed easily.
2. Mix the salt and pepper tighter evenly in a small bowl.
3. Put the pieces of pork belly in the mixture and toss them for even coating.
4. Preheat your air fryer for about 3 minutes
5. Now, put the pieces of pork in your air fryer basket.
6. Set the temperature to about 390 degrees F and cook the pork for about 15 minutes, but make sure you turn them over every 5 minutes.
7. After 15 minutes, they should be crispy and done.
8. Sometimes, they may take a little longer, or they could take less than 15 minutes. That's why you need to keep checking them every 5 minutes.
9. Drain them on paper towels. Now, you can serve them either hot or warm. Enjoy your tasty meal. You can add more spices to yours. Cooking requires being creative.

Nutrition Info:

- Protein: 26g Fiber: Negligible amount Carbohydrates: Very small Amount Sodium: 635mg Cholesterol: 95mg Unsaturated Fat:15g Saturated Fat: 9g Total Fat: 24g Calories: 332

Chicken Lettuce Wraps

Ingredients:

- 2 tablespoons of soy sauce
- 2 tablespoons of maple syrup or honey
- 2 green onions sprigs, chopped
- 2 garlic cloves, minced
- 1/4 cup of cold water
- 1/2 tablespoon of cornstarch
- 1/2 inch of knob ginger, minced
- 1.5 lbs of chicken breast, diced
- 1 tablespoon of rice vinegar
- 1 tablespoon of avocado or any oil
- 1 small zucchini, diced
- 1 small onion, finely chopped
- 1 small bell pepper, diced
- 1 head of butter, iceberg or Romaine lettuce
- 1 cup of cashew, coarsely chopped

Directions:

1. Fry the cashew until it is toasted. Then, you can transfer it into a bowl.
2. Add garlic, ginger, and onion to the cashew and cook the mixture in your air fryer for a minute or two. Make sure you keep stirring it as you cook.
3. Now, you can add the chicken before you cook for another 10 minutes. Stirring should never cease until you remove the chicken.
4. After the chicken has been cooked for 8 minutes, make a mixture of cornstarch, rice vinegar, maple syrup, soy sauce, and cold water in a small bowl and add the mixture to the almost-done chicken. Also, you can add bell pepper and zucchini to the mixture and cook for 2 minutes. The sauce should be thicker by now.
5. Add green onions and cashew to it. You can now serve the meal with stacked lettuce leaves.

Nutrition Info:

- Calories: 328 Potassium: 15% Total Fat: 15.8g Cholesterol: 82.7mg Sodium: 396.5mg Total Carbohydrates: 16g Dietary Fiber: 2g Protein: 31.2g

4-Week Meal Plan

Week 1

	Breakfast	Lunch	Dinner
Day 1	Santa Fe Style Pizza	Diet Boiled Ribs	Air Fried Section And Tomato
Day 2	Pancakes	Stuffed Chicken	Chicken Mushroom Stroganoff
Day 3	Cream Buns With Strawberries	Potatoes With Loin And Cheese	Fried Avocado
Day 4	Bruschetta	Air Fried Steak With Asparagus Bundles	Dark Chocolate Almond Yogurt Cups
Day 5	Misto Quente	Fish And Vegetable Tacos	Lighter Fish And Chips
Day 6	Cauliflower Hash Browns	Homemade Flamingos	Chocolate Chip Muffins
Day 7	Sweet Nuts Butter	Air Fry Rib-eye Steak	Fruity Coconut Energy Balls

Week 2

	Breakfast	Lunch	Dinner
Day 1	Grilled Cheese	Pork Head Chops With Vegetables	Creamy Halibut
Day 2	Scotch Eggs	Scallops With Green Vegetables	Mini Turkey Meatballs
Day 3	Zucchini Bread	Beef With Sesame And Ginger	Air Fried Pickle Chips
Day 4	Tofu Scramble	Salmon Spring Rolls	Carrot Ginger Soup
Day 5	Morning Mini Cheeseburger Sliders	Air Fryer Steak	Cinnamon Toasted Almonds
Day 6	Blueberry Buns	Salmon On Bed Of Fennel And Carrot	Mini Apple Oat Muffins
Day 7	Blueberry Muffins	Pork Fillets With Serrano Ham	Rustic Pear Pie With Nuts

Week 3

	Breakfast	Lunch	Dinner
Day 1	Grilled Sandwich With Three Types Of Cheese	Double Cheeseburger	Buffalo Cauliflower Wings
Day 2	Air Fried Sausage	Pork On A Blanket	Blistered Shishito Peppers
Day 3	Fried Egg	North Carolina Style Pork Chops	Tex-mex Salmon Stir-fry
Day 4	Stir-fried Broccoli Stalks	Air Fryer Beef Steak Kabobs With Vegetables	Roasted Vegetable Chicken Salad
Day 5	Bacon Bbq	Roasted Pork	Strawberry Lime Pudding
Day 6	Avocado Taco Fry	Pork Trinoza Wrapped In Ham	Warm Chicken And Spinach Salad
Day 7	Cinnamon And Cheese Pancake	Marinated Loin Potatoes	Grain-free Berry Cobbler

Week 4

	Breakfast	Lunch	Dinner
Day 1	Cocotte Eggs	Beef Scallops	Sweet Potato Chips
Day 2	Broccoli Mash	Snapper With Fruit	Lemony Yogurt Pound Cake
Day 3	Bagels	Steak	Two-bean Beef Chili
Day 4	French Toast In Sticks	Mustard-crusted Fish Fillets	Spaghetti Squash Alfredo
Day 5	Baked Eggs	Air Fried Empanadas	Homemade Muffins
Day 6	Breakfast Pizza	Air Fryer Bacon	Cranberry And Lemon Muffins
Day 7	Stuffed French Toast	Meatloaf Reboot	Pumpkin Spice Snack Balls

Appendix : Recipes Index

Made in the USA
Las Vegas, NV
19 March 2025

19809072R00059